Jade Pearce & [...]

BJORK & BJORK'S
DESIRABLE DIFFICULTIES
IN ACTION

IN ACTION | EDITOR
SERIES | **TOM SHERRINGTON**

WITH ILLUSTRATIONS BY
OLIVER CAVIGLIOLI

A **WALKTHRUs** PRODUCTION

 JOHN CATT
FROM HODDER EDUCATION

Orders: please contact Hachette UK Distribution, Hely Hutchinson Centre, Milton Road, Didcot, Oxfordshire, OX11 7HH. Telephone: +44 (0)1235 827827. Email education@hachette.co.uk. Lines are open from 9 a.m. to 5 p.m., Monday to Friday.

ISBN: 9781915261588

© 2024 Jade Pearce & Isaac Moore
Illustrations by Oliver Caviglioli

First published in 2024 by
John Catt from Hodder Education,
An Hachette UK Company
15 Riduna Park, Station Road,
Melton, Woodbridge IP12 1QT
Telephone: +44 (0)1394 389850
www.johncatt.com

MIX
Paper | Supporting
responsible forestry
FSC™ C104740
www.fsc.org

SERIES FOREWORD

TOM SHERRINGTON

The idea for the *In Action* series was developed by John Catt's *Teaching WalkThrus* team after we saw how popular our *Rosenshine's Principles in Action* booklets proved to be. We realised that the same approach might support teachers to access the ideas of a range of researchers, cognitive scientists and educators. A constant challenge that we wrestle with in the world of teaching and education research is the significant distance between the formulation of a set of concepts and conclusions that might be useful to teachers and the moment when a teacher uses those ideas to teach their students in a more effective manner, thereby succeeding in securing deeper or richer learning. Sometimes so much meaning is lost along that journey, through all the communication barriers that line the road, that the implementation of the idea bears no relation to the concept its originator had in mind. Sometimes it's more powerful to hear from a teacher about how they implemented an idea than it is to read about the idea from a researcher or cognitive scientist directly – because they reduce that distance; they push some of those barriers aside.

In our *In Action* series, the authors and their collaborative partners are all teachers or school leaders close to the action in classrooms in real schools. Their strategies for translating their subjects' work into practice bring fresh energy to a powerful set of original ideas in a way that we're confident will support teachers with their professional learning and, ultimately, their classroom practice. In doing so, they are also paying their respects to the original researchers and their work. In education, as in so many walks of life, we are standing on the shoulders of giants. We believe that our selection of featured researchers and papers represents some of the most important work done in the field of education in recent times.

In this excellent book, the focus is on the work of two brilliant researchers, Robert and Elizabeth Bjork. Their fascinating and powerful concept of 'desirable difficulties' has been explored through multiple blogs and conference sessions over recent years but, in my experience, has still been a source of some confusion when it comes to implementation. For example, beyond the realm of controlled trials, what exactly do 'spaced practice' and 'interleaving' look like in practice? As the Bjorks say themselves in their foreword, this is where the expertise and experience of our teacher authors come into play.

Jade Pearce and Isaac Moore have done a superb job of wrestling with the theoretical concepts that constitute desirable difficulties, then setting out multiple ways in which they apply to specific concepts. Using their knowledge and enthusiasm for the research in combination with their experience in the classroom, together with some case studies from other specialist teachers, they explore the sense in which difficulties can be desirable. In essence, this comes down to placing gains in long-term deep learning above more shallow or superficial learning that comes when the process might seem more immediately satisfying. They clarify the interplay between the concepts of storage strength and retrieval strength in explaining how memory works and suggest multiple ways that teachers can vary the conditions of practice – a central element in the Bjorks' model. I'd like to congratulate them on this excellent addition to the *In Action* series and their persistence in the writing of the book when both of them have such full-on day jobs!

Finally, in producing this series, we would like to acknowledge the significant influence of the researchED movement run by Tom Bennett that started in 2013. I was present at the first conference and, having seen the movement grow over the intervening years, I feel that many of us, including several *In Action* authors, owe a significant debt of gratitude to researchED for providing the forum where teachers' and researchers' ideas and perspectives can be shared. We are delighted, therefore, to be contributing a share of the royalties to researchED to support them in their ongoing non-profit work.

FOREWORD

ROBERT A. BJORK AND ELIZABETH LIGON BJORK

The title of the authors' volume, *Desirable Difficulties in Action*, serves to remind the two of us that incorporating desirable difficulties into actual instruction and/or the self-management of one's own learning has proved to be no easy matter. Early on, 30 years or so ago, findings from our laboratory and other laboratories made clear the importance of an old distinction between *performance*, the ability of learners to produce a correct answer or a problem-solving procedure during the instructional process, and *learning*, as measured by the ability to sometime later, after the instructional process, produce that answer or procedure in contexts where it is needed. We found, however, when given a choice of learning strategies – such as (a) spacing rather than massing restudy opportunities; (b) practising retrieval processes rather than restudying; or (c) interleaving rather than massing the study or practice of the separate components of some to-be-learned material or skills – that participants tended to choose the less effective strategies.

With hindsight, it now seems a bit laughable that we thought that simply reporting our findings would get students and others to change the way they studied or practised. First of all, habits, especially long-term habits, are not easy to change, and how a given learner studies or practises may reflect the influences of past teachers or instructors who were themselves prone to interpreting current performance as a valid index of learning. In addition, while making and correcting errors is a key component of effective learning, it can be interpreted, instead, as reflecting a failure of the learning strategy, the instructor, or both.

What is needed, in addition to learners actually experiencing the long-term consequences of more effective versus less effective learning procedures, is what the authors provide in this book: namely, concrete examples of more effective and less effective study activities taken from the real world of instruction and learning.

TABLE OF CONTENTS

CHAPTER 1

MEMORY AND LEARNING

The cognitive science model of memory and learning

According to The Derek Bok Center for Teaching and Learning, memory is the retention of information over time. Memory is also the cognitive process of encoding, storing and retrieving prior knowledge. Learning can be defined as a permanent change in long-term memory. When knowledge is more or less permanent and transfer is possible, then we say learning has taken place.

For example, I can tell you the address of the house where I grew up from memory because I have been able to encode, store and retrieve it many times over a period of years. As this memory is now more or less permanent, I have learned my childhood home address. When we are able to store and retrieve discrete but related knowledge, we begin to form knowledge connections. This enables us to use knowledge in lots of different ways and in different contexts.

Cognitive science has given us a model of memory and how learning occurs. This model, represented in the illustration below, shows that there are three components to learning:

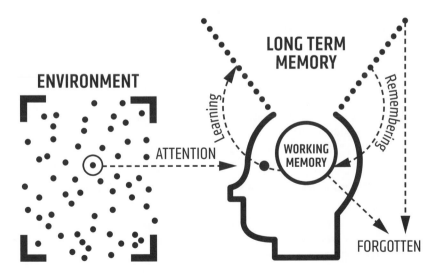

- **Attention:** Paying attention is the beginning of the learning process for our students. Attention is the gateway for information to pass from the environment into our working memory. The learning environment is full of information, some of which is unhelpful to learning. It is therefore important for class teachers to direct the attention of their students to what students need to learn.

- **Working memory:** Our working memory is where the information that has been collected by paying attention is processed. This is where thinking takes place. Our working memory is limited in both capacity and duration. Our current understanding is that working memory can only hold between four and seven items when dealing with a new situation. The capacity of working memory can be increased by retrieving information stored in long-term memory.

- **Long-term memory (LTM):** Long-term memory is where knowledge storage and integration take place. When we encounter new situations, information stored in our LTM can be recalled into our working memory to help us make sense of the new situation. Our LTM includes both episodic memories of personal events and semantic memories of facts and knowledge about subjects and the world. When we have actively processed information in our working memory, it is transferred to the LTM.

Five principles of learning

There are five principles from the cognitive science model of memory and learning that all teachers need to know about and plan for in their teaching to ensure that all students learn.

Principle 1: We learn only when we pay attention and think hard

We can only transfer new knowledge to the LTM if it first enters the working memory. Attention is required for this to happen. This shows the importance of limiting distractions and creating calm and orderly environments. However, this is not enough for students to learn. 'Memory is the residue of thought' (Willingham, 2009), so if we want our students to remember complex content, they have to think about the materials. There is no learning without thinking.

Principle 2: Our working memory is limited when we learn something new

The amount of new information that we are able to process at any one time in working memory is limited. If the capacity of the working memory is overloaded, the transfer to the LTM is impeded and so learning is hindered. This means it is crucial for teachers to limit the amount of new content students are asked to process at any one time. Teachers can do this by chunking, removing redundant information and using images or diagrams alongside verbal explanations.

Principle 3: What we know determines what we learn and how quickly we learn

The prior knowledge that our students have in their LTM enables them to make sense of new concepts and situations that they encounter during teaching. But this prior knowledge is not the same for all students. Therefore it is important that class teachers are able to check this and support students to modify it before introducing something new. Doing this enhances how well and quickly students learn.

Principle 4: Fluency arises through practice over time

For students to develop fluency, there needs to be sufficient practice both in lessons and at home. This strengthens the storage of the content in the LTM and ensures it is retrievable in the future. When students are not fluent, what we teach them can be easily forgotten.

Principle 5: There is a relationship between learning and forgetting

It is common for forgetting to be seen as the enemy of learning, but the relationship between the two is not that simple. This is because allowing for some forgetting can often enhance learning. To learn (retain knowledge long term), there should be some forgetting. To forget, we should wait before we check for learning. Planned forgetting is therefore good for learning.

Summary

- Memory can be described as the cognitive process of encoding, storing and retrieving prior knowledge.

- When memory is more or less permanent, then we say learning has taken place.

- Attention is the gateway for information to pass from the environment into our working memory.

- Our working memory is where the information that has been collected by paying attention is processed. This is where thinking takes place.

- When we encounter a new situation, information stored in our LTM can be recalled into our working memory to help us make sense of the new situation.

- There are five principles from the cognitive science model of memory and learning that all teachers need to know about and plan for in their teaching to ensure that all students learn.

- To learn, there should be some forgetting. To forget, we should wait before we check for learning. Some forgetting, when planned, is a friend of learning.

CHAPTER 2

INTRODUCING DESIRABLE DIFFICULTIES

Learning versus performance

To understand desirable difficulties, we first need to understand the distinction between performance and learning. **Performance** is what we can observe during or soon after instruction. For example, a teacher is teaching a class about electric current. After explaining what current is and why current moves around a circuit, the teacher then proceeds to ask questions. All students correctly answer the questions. This is performance. However, the ability of students to answer these questions does not mean they have learned. We still would not be able to say they have learned if they did well in a test completed immediately or days after they have been taught about electric current.

As stated previously, **learning** is a more permanent change in knowledge or understanding. This may be seen in an assessment completed days, weeks or even months later. This definition of learning is important for the choices that teachers make in their lessons as it means that we should choose strategies that are more effective for learning over those that improve performance.

This distinction is also supported by the concept of **latent learning** – learning that only becomes clear when a student has an incentive to show the knowledge (for example, in assessments and external exams) but is not seen in improvements in performance.

Honzik and Tolman (1936) carried out an experiment in which three groups of rats were placed in a complex maze over a period of 17 days. One group of rats was given no reward for reaching the target until the 11th day. A second group was never rewarded for reaching the target but taken out of the maze when they reached the target. A third group of rats was rewarded every time they reached the target.

The results of the experiment showed that the group of rats that was regularly rewarded made the fewest errors. The group of rats that was not rewarded made the most errors. The group of rats that was not rewarded until day 11 made the same number of errors as the never-rewarded group until day 11, after which they were rewarded for finding the target. The number of errors made then dropped significantly. This third group of rats did learn even without any reward and without showing gains in performance.

Latent learning is also possible in humans. Stevenson (1954) showed that considerable learning can take place in humans without changes to performance. In this experiment, children were tasked with finding a key that would open a box. There were other non-key objects in the environment during this task. When the children were subsequently asked to find the position of these non-key objects, they were relatively faster in locating them. Latent learning occurred during their search for the key that would open the box.

Retrieval strength and storage strength

In 'A new theory of disuse and an old theory of stimulus fluctuation', Bjork and Bjork (1992) proposed that there are two strengths to memory, namely storage and retrieval strength. Storage strength is a measure of how well learned knowledge is and how likely it is to be retrieved in the future. The storage strength of a memory increases as a function of opportunities for retrieval. As many items as possible can be stored in long-term memory as there is no limit on storage capacity. Retrieval strength on the other hand is a measure of the current ease of access to knowledge in memory. Retrieval strength is demonstrated by current performance like answering questions in lessons. This is performance and not learning.

Storage strength increases when we allow retrieval strength to decrease over a period of time through forgetting. It is therefore important for teachers to focus on improving storage strength for their students. This is what learning is about.

What are desirable difficulties?

The idea of **desirable difficulty** describes strategies that slow down performance but enhance long-term learning. These strategies or practices are desirable because they require students to think hard and so enhance long-term retention and knowledge transfer – they increase learning. However, they are difficult because they are challenging and slow down the rate at which a learner's performance improves.

In the seminal paper 'Making things hard on yourself but in a good way: creating desirable difficulties to enhance learning' by Bjork and Bjork (2011), the following are the four desirable difficulties:

1. Spacing
2. Varying the conditions of practice
3. Interleaving
4. Testing.

Undesirable difficulties

It should be noted here that not all difficulties are desirable. **Undesirable difficulties** make the initial processing of the new content more challenging without leading to gains in long-term learning. There are a number of potential undesirable difficulties including:

1. Asking learners to engage with new content without the necessary background knowledge to do so – for example, through discovery learning or using trial and error to solve problems. For learners to think hard there needs to be some knowledge to think with. If learners do not have the background knowledge needed to engage with desirable difficulties strategies, we expose them to undesirable difficulties.

2. Any instruction that causes cognitive overload or makes the initial presentation of the new content more difficult. This is explained more later.

In their paper, Chen et al. (2018) looked into why desirable difficulties (DD) effects are not always realised and suggested cognitive load theory as a way to explain the variability in the effects that have been observed. They specifically named high element interactivity as a cause of the loss of the DD effects. Interactive elements are defined as 'elements that must be processed simultaneously in working memory as they are logically related'. Element interactivity can be determined by 'estimating the number of interacting elements in learning materials' (Sweller, 2010).

In their chapter in *Advances in Cognitive Load Theory*, Leahy and Sweller defined element interactivity as 'a measure of complexity that is central to cognitive load theory'. It considers the characteristics of the information being processed and the knowledge held in the learner's long-term memory. By taking both factors into consideration, teachers can teach in a way that reduces working-memory load to support the transfer of information to long-term memory. A high element interactivity creates the kind of difficulty for learners that is undesirable. It is about working-memory load, not the level of difficulty of what is being taught.

The implications of element interactivity for teachers and teaching practice include the following:

- When material is easy for students to understand, students should generate their own models or responses, rather than be shown them. Materials may be easy to understand either because there is low element interactivity or because previously high element interactivity material has been learned and incorporated into knowledge in long-term memory.

- The use of worked examples is effective for materials high in element interactivity. As the level of learner expertise increases, the level of element interactivity decreases. The generation effect should take over at this point. This means that when students' level of expertise has reached a certain level determined by the teacher's expertise, students should be asked to generate responses.

- Undesirable difficulties prevent students from succeeding. Students need to succeed eventually or else any difficulty introduced as part of the learning process is undesirable. It is important to reinstate that being successful starts when students encounter the material for the first time. Securing attention, element interactivity and overlearning are all essential first steps in the classroom.

Summary

- Performance is the gain in understanding demonstrated during or soon after instruction. Learning is a long-term change in knowledge or understanding.

- Considerable learning can occur in humans without changes in performance or reinforcement.

- Memory can be characterised by two strengths – storage strength and retrieval strength.

- Storage strength increases when we allow retrieval strength to decrease over a period of time through forgetting.

- Desirable difficulties are strategies that impede immediate performance but enhance long-term learning. This is because they require students to think hard and engage in more in-depth processing.

- Desirable difficulties include spacing, varying the conditions of practice, interleaving and testing.

- Not all difficulties are desirable. Undesirable difficulties make the initial processing of the new content more challenging without leading to gains in long-term learning. They should be avoided.

CHAPTER 3

DESIRABLE DIFFICULTY 1: SPACING

What is spacing and why is it a desirable difficulty?

The practice of spacing out restudy opportunities rather than completing these in immediate succession is known as spacing. This has been shown in numerous studies to promote long-term retention, which is essential for learning (Vlach and Sandhofer, 2013). Compared to massed practice, the advantages of spacing are significant (Bjork and Bjork, 2011).

Spacing is desirable because the delay between study and revisiting induces forgetting, which improves long-term knowledge retention, comprehension and knowledge transfer. However, allowing for forgetting reduces performance and makes learning feel more challenging for students. This is why spacing is a desirable difficulty.

What research supports spacing?

In this section, we present results from some of the many experiments and studies that provide evidence of the benefit of spacing to learning. The duration between first study and restudy of the same material is known as 'gap' while the duration between restudy and final test is known as 'retention interval' (RI).

A new theory of disuse and an old theory of stimulus fluctuation

In this paper, Bjork and Bjork (1992) theorised on the benefits of spacing out repeated study trials on long-term retention. They explained that the spacing of study or practice results in higher storage strength than does massing of practice. This is because retrieval strength fades over time, and due to the negative relationship between retrieval strength and gains in storage strength, this results in stronger storage and therefore improved long-term retention.

The Forgetting Curve

Ebbinghaus's Forgetting Curve demonstrates that after initial learning, the amount of newly learned content that students can recall falls over time. However, if we re-encounter the material after a delay, we will retain more of the content for a longer time period. This suggests that spacing practice out can aid long-term learning.

Roediger and Karpicke

Roediger and Karpicke (2011) carried out a series of experiments involving challenging vocabulary that was learned under different conditions. These conditions included mass practice, expanding spacing and uniform spacing. They found that a single test taken shortly after instruction produced better recall than a test with a longer delay on the same day. In a test carried out two days later, the delayed test schedule produced better recall. Both the expanding and uniform spacing schedules produced better recall than the mass practice schedule.

Furthermore, the expanding spacing schedule recalled more items initially than the uniform spacing schedule for repeat testing. However, there was a reversal in recall performance after two days: uniform spacing produced better long-term retention than expanding spacing. Why was there a reversal? Uniform spacing involves a delay (usually days) to the first test. This delay is good for long-term knowledge retention. In the case of expanding spacing, the first test is often too close to the first time students are taught information. Retrieval strength is therefore higher, and this has a detrimental effect on storage strength.

Latimier, Peyre and Ramus

Latimier, Peyre and Ramus (2021) carried out a meta-analysis of 29 studies that investigated the effect of spacing out retrieval practice on final retention. They compared the strengths of massed practice, expanding spacing and uniform spacing schedules. The results from one of their experiments showed that spaced retrieval practice schedules are better for long-term recall than massed practice.

Another set of results from their work showed no significant difference between expanding and uniform spacing schedules. They found that the more learners are tested, the more beneficial the expanding spacing schedule is, but there is no significant difference between expanding and uniform spacing schedules.

Cepeda et al.

Cepeda et al. (2008) reported the results of a comprehensive set of study and testing episodes involving 1354 students. They claimed that 'this was the most systematic analysis of long-term spacing effects carried out at the time'. They combined various gaps and RI (retention interval) values for a total of 26 different conditions. The gaps used in this study were 0, 1, 7, 21, 35, 70 and 105 days. For RIs, they investigated 7, 35, 70 and 350 days.

The results showed that for each RI, final performance initially rose with increasing gap and then fell as the gap increased further. As the RI increased, the ratio between the gap and the RI decreased. The optimum gap increases but not at the same rate as the RI. For the RIs of 7, 35, 70 and 350 days, the optimal gaps were 1, 11, 21 and 23 days respectively for recall and 1, 7, 7 and 21 days respectively for recognition.

Is there an optimally efficient gap between study sessions? It turns out that the optimal gap can only be determined by how long we want our students to retain knowledge. Cepeda and his co-researchers concluded: 'If you want to know the optimal distribution of your study time, you need to decide how long you wish to remember something for.'

Limitations of spacing

The initial gap between study and initial testing puts a limit on the spacing effect

Verkoeijen, Rikers and Schmidt (2005) showed that the relationship between free recall and spacing gap 'follows an inverted U-shaped function'. They considered both incidental and intentional processing during instruction. Incidental means that processing during instruction was shallow, while intentional means that processing was deep. In both incidental and intentional learning conditions, if we continue to increase the spacing gap, free recall will increase up to a maximum and then a further increase in spacing gap leads to less successful recall.

The quality of learning instruction influences the spacing effect

Verkoeijen, Rikers and Schmidt (2005) investigated the effect of the depth of processing on the relationship between spacing and recall. They showed that intentional learning (deep processing) was more effective for recall than incidental processing for all the different gaps investigated. Their results also showed that retention lasts longer in intentional than in incidental processing. The quality of instruction therefore places a limit on the effectiveness of spacing.

Limited evidence from applications in primary classrooms

Goossens et al. (2016) looked into the effectiveness of spacing on vocabulary recall as part of the primary curriculum. The children carried out six tasks spaced within one week or across two weeks. For each repetition, the children either restudied or recalled the description. After one to 11 weeks, the children were tested using a multiple-choice vocabulary test and cued recall tests. No benefit was found on either cued recall or the multiple-choice test. These results put into question the effectiveness of spacing in primary school settings.

However, the work of Carpenter, Pan and Butler (2022) showed that spacing is beneficial for long-term knowledge retention for elementary age children (5–7 years) and middle school age children (9–11 years). This supports the idea that spacing works for all age ranges of students.

Implementing spacing in the classroom

How long a gap should be left before revisiting?

The optimal gap to first restudy can be best determined by deciding how long we want our students to remember something. For example, if we want Year 10 students to remember a topic by the time they write their GCSE exams at the end of Year 11, then we will need to know the number of days between teaching the topic and the date the knowledge will be tested in the final exam.

Extrapolated gap (days)	Retention intervals (days)	Days from study until final test
3	7	10
8	35	43
12	70	82
27	350	377

Table 3.1 Extrapolated gap and retention interval from Cepeda et al. (2008).

Table 3.1 indicates that if you teach students a topic today, for which there will be a test in 10 days' time, the optimum restudy should be on day 3.

The data in Table 3.1 is shown as a graph in Figure 3.1.

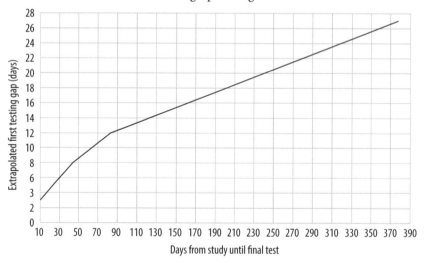

Figure 3.1 Graph showing the relationship between days from study until final test and gap to first retrieval or restudy.

Curriculum planning and implementation

All of the research cited shows that spacing needs to be planned into the curriculum so that it is implemented by all teachers as effectively as possible. An example of this curriculum planning in KS3 science can be seen in Table 3.2.

Sequence	Year 7	Year 8	Year 9
1	Energy	Conduction, convection and radiation	Respiration
2	Forces and gravity	Space 1: the universe and stars	Space 2: detecting stars using waves
3	Particles (atomic)	Atoms/electron configuration/ions	Acids and bases
4	Elements and compounds	Why chemical reactions happen – incomplete shells and atoms rearrangement	Energy changes during reactions
5	Particle model	Series and parallel circuits	Electromagnetism
6	Cells/tissues/organs	Photosynthesis	Ecology
7	Reproduction in humans	Reproduction in plants	Inheritance

Table 3.2 A possible curriculum sequence in KS3 science.

Table 3.3 shows how this curriculum could incorporate effective spacing.

Topic	Date topic is completed	Gap between topic completion and a final test (days)	Gap between topic completion and first test/restudy (days)	Second restudy opportunity calculated from the first test (days)
Energy	September 29	249	21	21
Forces and gravity	October 20	228	20	19
Particles (atomic)	November 30	187	18	17
Elements and compounds	January 12	144	17	15
Particle model and properties	February 9	116	15	14
Cells/tissues/organs	March 15	81	13	12
Reproduction in humans	May 24	11	10	0

Table 3.3 An example of a Year 7 science knowledge sequence showing two opportunities for retrieval of the same content.

The delay to the first retrieval is the most important factor in any spacing schedule. If the delay is too short, retrieval will not be as effortful as it should be.

If the delay is too long, students may forget all they have been taught. Effortful retrieval is essential to long-term retention. If you need to change the delays, go longer and not shorter. A level of flexibility is needed around the number of days for delayed restudy.

How many spacing opportunities are needed? Multiple repeats of the same content are needed to support long-term retention. In Table 3.3, the first retrieval opportunity is taken as the first study and a new delay (second restudy opportunity) is calculated using the graph in Figure 3.1. The amount of spaced testing/restudy you can implement will depend on the workload associated with marking, the amount of content still to be taught and the combination of different relearning methods (spaced homework, cumulative tests, lesson revisits and testing). Many testing or restudy episodes need to be planned into the curriculum. This is because final test performance improves as the amount of restudy/testing increases, as long as the testing is effortful. The graph in Figure 3.1 can be used to plan as much restudy/testing as possible into the curriculum. Content selection is therefore important as you may not be able to teach all content in your curriculum.

Spaced homework

One of the ways to implement multiple spacing in your curriculum is through the use of spaced or lagged homework. Here, homework is based not on current learning but on previously learned content. This may include spaced retrieval practice, revisiting content through reading or a task that requires students to revisit prior learning. If using spaced homework, it is important that all students complete the homework and teachers give feedback to all students.

Cumulative tests

Tests that include questions not just on the content that has been studied recently, but also on materials that were learned in previous weeks, months and years encourage students to revisit this content in the tests and in their independent preparation. Care needs to be taken to ensure that cumulative tests cover all of the important knowledge that students need to do well in their final exams.

For example, the final test in Table 3.3 can be a cumulative test set for the end of term. The cumulative test is then treated as a study episode and a new delay calculated for an end-of-year assessment if needed. New topics after the cumulative test follow a new spacing schedule.

Revisit lessons

For the most complex concepts, it may be beneficial to reteach this material after a delay. This can include the teacher giving another explanation of the content and pupils completing further practice tasks, questions and activities.

Within topic/unit spacing

In addition to the spacing that is done once a topic or unit has been completed, teachers should also consider implementing spacing when teaching a topic or unit. This is often done using spaced retrieval opportunities. Previously taught content within the unit is retrieved before new knowledge is introduced and the retrieval is spaced. This type of spacing within topics or units is more effective if the sequence of questions supports how we want our students to develop connections between the different knowledge within the topic or unit.

Summary

- Spacing is when learning episodes are spread out over time as opposed to occurring all at once, as in massed practice.

- Spacing makes the learning process more challenging as between each episode some forgetting occurs. However, this forgetting also allows for greater gains in storage strength and so supports long-term retention.

- The optimal delay between learning episodes depends on the gap between first encountering the material and the final test. The longer the delay to the final test, the longer the delay to the first restudy or test up to a maximum.

- It is important that the first revisit is not too soon after the initial learning in order to ensure the first recall is challenging.

- The effectiveness of spacing depends on the quality of instruction when students first encounter learning materials.

- Spacing should be planned into the curriculum.

- Spacing can be achieved through reteaching previously learned content in a later lesson, spaced homework, spaced retrieval practice and cumulative tests.

Case study of the use of spacing in secondary English

Amy Coombe, school improvement lead at Athena Learning Trust

One of the biggest challenges in the English classroom is supporting students to write analytically about a text. To write analytically, students need to have a deep understanding of the text, plus have the vocabulary with which to articulate their ideas, alongside knowledge of how to write. To tackle this challenge, my team and I have pinned down what within the text, from the seemingly infinite options, should be prioritised within our teaching. Next, we sequenced this knowledge carefully, and we revisit it deliberately so that it will be remembered. Without this knowledge at their fingertips, students are unable to write well.

We ensure that deliberate revisiting of knowledge occurs within units. For example, when teaching Charles Dickens's *A Christmas Carol*, symbolism is revisited multiple times. It is first taught after reading the text, after encountering Victorian context, and after exploring Dickens's portrayal of Scrooge's miserly character. At this stage, students understand enough about these areas in order to explore Dickens's use of Scrooge's actions, words and choices to symbolise attitudes towards the poor in Victorian society. It is then revisited in relation to these characters:

- Bob Cratchit: a symbol of poverty, representing the poor in Victorian society.
- Fred: a symbol of charity, representing kindness and forgiveness.
- Fezziwig: a symbol of goodness, representing the kind middle classes.
- Ignorance and Want: symbols of the poor.
- Tiny Tim: a symbol of the experiences of the most vulnerable.
- The novella: a symbol of our responsibility to others.

Planning this revisiting deliberately has ensured that our students encounter the concept of symbolism enough, in different and meaningful contexts, to deeply understand it. Each time the concept is revisited, there is an opportunity to dive deeper and challenge our students further. As a result, **all** students are able to write confidently about Dickens's use of symbolism to convey his ideas about Victorian society.

We've also sequenced recaps of quotations, vocabulary, character actions and contextual ideas for the entire unit and completed a tally to check that each concept is revisited enough. This deliberate revisiting has helped **all** of our students remember in **every** classroom; none of this is left up to chance. It enables us to revisit the most versatile knowledge more often; it enables deeper retrieval each time knowledge is revisited.

Similarly, we have planned revisiting of knowledge across the whole of the English curriculum. For example, concepts such as symbolism are introduced in Year 7 and revisited each year in different and deeper contexts, alongside other useful vocabulary, such as 'explores', 'exposes', 'evokes', 'criticises' and 'challenges', which support students in developing and articulating interpretations of the writer's purpose. Not only do we teach these words explicitly, but we revisit them deliberately and often within recaps and within the body of the lesson multiple times over the course of the curriculum. The result is that our students remember them and are able to use them adeptly within their speech and writing.

CHAPTER 4
DESIRABLE DIFFICULTY 2: VARYING CONDITIONS OF PRACTICE

What is 'varying the conditions of practice' and why is it a desirable difficulty?

When learning becomes contextualised, the material may be easily retrieved in the familiar context, but students may struggle to retrieve the material if tested in a different context or after some delay or both (Bjork and Bjork, 2011). In contrast, changing the context of instruction helps students to broaden their knowledge and skills and to use them more flexibly. This can include the physical environmental setting – for example, the room in which learning takes place, the time of the learning, the way materials are presented or the examples and explanations that are provided.

When practice is structured such that the conditions, type of materials or tasks remain the same, processing requirements stay much the same, increasing the apparent rate of acquisition but not leading to the deep processing required for long-term retention. To vary the conditions of practice is to make the conditions under which instruction occurs unpredictable. Doing this creates difficulties for students and performance suffers as a consequence. Students do not like this. But as varying the conditions of practice supports long-term retention of knowledge, it is therefore desirable.

What research supports varying the conditions of practice?

Many studies have shown that changing the context of the learning environment can enhance long-term retention. Such results have been obtained in verbal learning tasks (Mannes and Kintsch, 1987), problem solving (Gick and Holyoak, 1980) and concept learning (Homa and Cultice, 1984). We summarise some of these studies in this chapter.

Environmental context and human memory

In a study by Bjork (1975), students were presented with a list of 40 vocabulary words, which were repeated after a three-hour interval either in the same room or in a different room. The mode of presentation was also different in these rooms. Students were then tested for free recall in a neutral room after an additional three-hour interval. Students that were given instructions in the same room recalled fewer words compared to students that were given their instructions in two different rooms.

An advance organiser that facilitates learning but not remembering

In a study by Mannes and Kintsch (1987), students were given some materials on background knowledge about microbes before reading a technical article on the use of microbes in the industry. Not all the information in the background material was relevant to the technical article. The background material was presented in two ways – in one presentation, the background material was organised in the same format as the article and in the other presentation, the format of the background material was different.

Presenting the background material in the same format as the article led to better free recall and sentence verification. When the background material was presented in a different format to the article, students made better inferences and performed better in a problem-solving task. Presenting the material in a different format led to better overall performance.

The effects of environmental context on the recall of information

Alonso and Fernandez (2011) changed the physical context in which both study and testing were done. Students learned a list of words in one room and were tested in another room. One group of students was also asked to notice the layout of the room while learning, but the same instruction was not given to the other group. Changing the context did affect retrieval as it caused longer retention time (weeks and months). Their experiments also seem to indicate that for long retention intervals, putting extra effort into memorising the layout of the room during encoding supports better recall of what has been learned when the test is subsequently carried out in a different room.

Effects of environmental context manipulated by the combination of place and task on free recall

Isarida and Isarida (2004) carried out three experiments to investigate the effect of context on free recall of nouns with a retention interval of 10 minutes. In the first experiment, the room and task were both changed. In the second experiment, only the room was changed and in the third experiment, only the task was changed. The experiment in which both room and task were changed produced the best free recall.

Implementing varied conditions of practice in the classroom

Homework

Having a spacing schedule that involves students practising in school and at home is one way for teachers to vary the physical environmental context in a meaningful way. Take, for example, a department that implements a spacing schedule that involves spaced or lagged homework. In lessons, the teacher gives students the opportunity to attempt questions during independent practice. At the end of this part of practice, the class teacher sets the remaining questions to be completed at home some days after this initial practice. In a lesson on or soon after the submission date, the teacher goes through the answers to the questions and gives feedback. In this example, the physical environment of the practice has changed. This amounts to varying the conditions of practice.

Varying the use of cues in practice sessions

Cued recall refers to recalling information using cues and guides. It can help students to remember material they would not remember in free recall. There is more chance of recalling an item when it has a strong link with the cue. However, strong performance during practice may not help long-term retention of knowledge, especially when such cues are not present during testing. Varying the cues provided during practice can mean students' ability to recall information is not dependent on a specific cue. For example, when teaching gravitational potential energy (GPE) in science, we could provide a cue in the form of images or in the form of the equation for GPE.

Varying the type of questions we ask

Varying the conditions of practice is important if the situation in which knowledge will be applied is unpredictable. This is especially true if what is to be learned is complex or conceptual. To adequately prepare students for these situations, we can vary the type of questions we ask in lessons. In science, students may be asked to define a concept, combine knowledge of two or more concepts to solve a problem, use information presented in a table or graph and use equations to solve problems. The type of questions we ask can support students to generalise their understanding of a concept and use knowledge flexibly. In maths, an effective way to do this is through the application of variation theory, in terms of both conceptual and procedural variation. This is discussed in the case study at the end of the chapter.

Varying the structure of teaching materials

Many teachers use past exam papers to help students prepare for exams. This is often the case when students take mock exams. Teachers can vary the conditions of practice by ensuring that the format of the mock exam questions does not match the format of the questions in the final exam. How preparation questions are presented can be varied too. For example, some questions can be written by teachers, rather than taken from past papers. Questions in assessments may be organised by topic or randomly spread across the assessment paper.

Summary

- To vary the conditions of practice is to make the conditions under which instruction occurs unpredictable.
- Varying the conditions of practice worsens performance in the short term but supports long-term retention of knowledge.
- Varying the conditions of practice is especially beneficial when learning complex or conceptual content.
- Changing the context of instruction or study helps students to broaden their knowledge and skills and to use them more flexibly.
- Changing the location of study, time of study, how study episodes are organised, spacing delays, the type of questions we ask students and interleaving are all examples of how to change the conditions of practice.
- The use of variation theory in some subjects is a way of introducing both conceptual and procedural variations.

Case study of the use of variation in maths

Peter Williams, head of maths at Crown Hills Community College

Here are two examples of different task structures that show off the power of variation. First, a very simple true/false task:

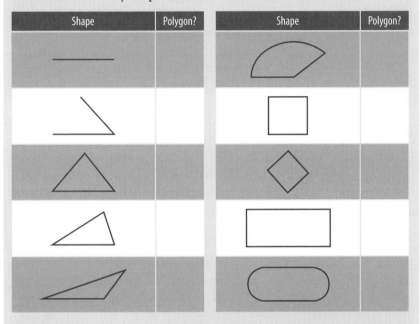

Used with permission from Craig Barton. Source: https://variationtheory.com/2018/08/03/what-is-a-polygon/

This is a key step in carefully defining a new concept, but showing students many different variations, some of which represent the concept and some of which deliberately do not. These are often referred to as examples and non-examples. The task would involve me walking through a shape at a time, explaining why it is or isn't a polygon. Then the students would get a smaller set of similar shapes to decide for themselves, to check they understood the concept clearly.

The second structure is a completion table:

a	b	$a+b$	$a-b$	$a \times b$	$a \div b$
6×10^{17}	2×10^{17}				
	2×10^{17}	6×10^{17}			
	2×10^{17}		6×10^{17}		
	2×10^{17}			6×10^{34}	
	2×10^{17}				6
6×10^{18}	2×10^{17}				
4×10^{-13}	5×10^{-14}				
	5×10^{-14}	4×10^{-13}			
	5×10^{-14}		4×10^{-13}		
	5×10^{-14}			4×10^{-26}	
	5×10^{-14}				4
4×10^{-12}	5×10^{-14}				

Used with permission from Nathan Day. Source: https://interwovenmaths.com/standardformcalculations

This is used after a concept has been taught as a way of giving students structured but increasingly challenging practice. The same skill is being tested throughout, but working backwards as well as forwards, and with similarity between the rows to help students notice key features of the skill.

Generally, the class teacher explains the task, gives students a few minutes to get started, then pauses them and asks them to complete the first row as a class to check they have understood. After that, it's lots of circulating and supporting. I have found that these tasks always engage classes well because they start nice and easy, but if designed well, they can really stretch students' thinking.

Varying the type of questions we ask students makes learning flexible, and flexible learning supports knowledge transfer as it is done under different contexts. The application of variation theory allows teachers to accomplish just this. Next is a case study from an English teacher on how varying the context of the use of vocabulary can support flexible knowledge.

Case study of variation theory and deep processing in English

Jennifer Webb, assistant principal, responsible for
teaching and learning at Trinity Academy

Variation is a pedagogical tool that highlights the essential features of a concept by demonstrating and exploring varied examples and non-examples of that concept. Much of the research in this area comes from the discipline of maths, but there are powerful potential applications in English.

At my school, we teach new vocabulary using a process we have developed called the 'Quick Vocabulary Method'. The core of this method involves showing a range of examples and non-examples of the word used in different sentences. For each of these examples, students use mini-whiteboards to indicate whether the word is being used correctly or not. This enables us to show students how a word might be used in different contexts, and in different grammatical forms, while also teasing out common misconceptions and errors we know students are likely to make.

For example, the English department might teach the word *reinforce*. They might show the following examples:

The writer *reinforces* this idea by describing…	This is an example of the word used in the way the teacher might want students to use it in a literature essay.
The writer wants to *reinforce* this character as manipulative.	This is a non-example – it teases out a common error related to how to use certain analytical verbs.
Macbeth continues to order the murders of his subjects, *reinforcing* his power in Scotland.	This is an example of the word being used to describe something a character is doing, rather than just a writer. It is also written in a different grammatical form.
The ceiling was made of *reinforced* concrete.	This is a non-subject example, but demonstrates how the word might function outside of an English subject context. It is also using the word as an adjective, not a verb.

33

Each of these examples shows the ways in which this word can be used, and therefore gives students a broader understanding of it. If students are only ever shown the first example, they may not understand how it could function in other contexts.

The example here is relatively simple, but the principles can be extended to many of the most complex ideas in our subject. English is a subject that requires students to know things in many different ways. We want them to be able to define and explain something, but we also want them to be able to apply their knowledge with confidence, accuracy and fluency. A student, for instance, might be able to tell us what the active voice is, but we would also want them to:

- Tell us whether a new text is written in the active or passive voice
- Tell us the difference between the active and passive voice
- Tell us *why* someone might use the active voice
- Tell us the possible *effect(s)* of this grammatical choice on the text, the meaning or the reader
- Independently notice when a text is using active or passive voice without being prompted (this is very different to being directed to look for these features by a teacher)
- Make a conscious decision to use the active or passive voice in their own writing
- Use the active or passive voice in their own writing in a way that is *skilful* and *effective*
- Be empowered to work with this concept in a way that doesn't see it as a grammar *rule*, but in a way that is a choice and something they can use in novel and interesting ways.

Looking at this list of ways to know this concept in English, you can see how a student's deepening appreciation of a concept might be developed by continued re-exposure to it in a range of new contexts. Once I have taught the concept initially, I might deepen student understanding by showing an increasing range of examples in different contexts, such as an example in political writing versus one in literary fiction, or examples with different syntactical structures. The more students *see*, the deeper and broader their knowledge of the concept and all the things that concept might be.

CHAPTER 5

DESIRABLE DIFFICULTY 3: INTERLEAVING

What is interleaving and why is it a desirable difficulty?

Interleaving involves sequencing learning tasks so that similar items are interspersed with slightly different items (Perry et al., 2021). More specifically, interleaving includes the mixing together of different types of items, questions, problems (Karpicke and O'Day) or skills within a single practice session (Hughes and Lee, 2019). This is opposed to blocked practice, which involves practising several types of the same item or problem in a row.

Interleaving can be said to be a desirable difficulty because it impairs short-term performance in comparison to blocked practice. However, this initial difficulty increases processing, strengthening the long-term memory and resulting in much better retention on a delayed test (Bjork and Bjork, 2011).

Why is interleaving effective?

The discriminative-contrast hypothesis

The discriminative-contrast hypothesis states that interleaving is effective because it increases opportunities to compare and contrast examples, and so makes the differences between them more obvious, supporting students to discriminate between them (Birnbaum et al., 2013).

This hypothesis is supported by the research that has shown that interleaving increases retention, where temporal spacing (presenting examples in a blocked format but with short gaps of time between them) does not always do so. For example, Kang and Pashler (2012) tested participants' ability to identify the artist of specific paintings as a result of either interleaved practice, or blocked practice but with a time delay. They found that interleaving was beneficial over blocking, but temporally spaced blocking was not. Therefore, the benefit was due to interleaving not temporal spacing. This shows that it is the discrimination of examples that supports learning as opposed to spacing of examples because they are not presented consecutively (Brunmair and Richter, 2019).

The discriminative-contrast hypothesis also explains why studies that have interleaved unrelated items have not found this to be beneficial – there are no differences to note and so no benefits from increased discrimination between the items (Firth, Rivers and Boyle, 2021). For instance, Kornell and Bjork (2008) compared interleaving with similar material to interleaving with trivia questions to prevent contrast. They found that interleaving with trivia questions did not give the benefits of standard interleaved practice. This again supports the view that it is the opportunity to discriminate that makes interleaving effective.

Research has shown this to be particularly applicable to mathematics, as students must be able to select the correct method to solve similar problems. Interleaving similar mathematical problems helps students to discriminate between the problem types and their correct solutions, and so they become more effective at selecting the correct strategy (Perry et al., 2021). This has been shown to reduce discrimination errors when students select the wrong strategy (Taylor and Rohrer, 2010).

Retrieval practice

It may be that interleaving is effective, in part, due to the testing effect (the benefit tests or quizzes have on long-term retention, also known as retrieval practice). This is because interleaving means there is a delay in looking at the same type of content (due to the interspersing of slightly different examples), and students are therefore required to retrieve each part of the content each time they revisit it (Bjork and Bjork, 2011). In contrast to massed practice, the information will no longer be in students' short-term memories, therefore it has to be retrieved each time that aspect of the topic is revisited (Hughes and Lee, 2019).

What research supports interleaving?

Interleaving has been shown to be effective with a range of materials:

1. The learning of scientific words (such as *transcription, transduction, transformation,* and *translation*) with similar spelling and meanings (Rohrer, 2012).

2. The learning of motor skills. For example, Hall, Domingues and Cavazos (1994) found that later performance of college baseball players in pitching was better if interleaved practice of different pitches had been used.

3. In a seminal study in 2008, Kornell and Bjork found interleaving to be more effective than blocked practice when learning to identify the paintings of different artists. Participants that had studied using interleaving were more accurately able to identify the artist responsible for novel paintings in a later test. A recent review of 119 studies widened this, finding that interleaving practice was very effective for categorisation learning when categories were highly similar to one another (Chen, Paas and Sweller, 2021).

4. As explained earlier, numerous studies have demonstrated that interleaving is particularly effective for learning in maths. Rohrer and Taylor (2007) examined the impact of interleaved practice in comparison to blocked practice when learning how to calculate the volume of different shapes. Interleaving practice resulted in participants being able to correctly solve more problems in a test one week later compared to those who completed blocked practice – 63% compared to 20%. Taylor and Rohrer replicated this in a later study (2010) with interleaving proving more effective when children practised four types of maths problems. Children in the interleaving group were more likely to choose the correct method to solve the problem and produce the correct response, and less likely to attempt to use the wrong strategy (10% used the wrong strategy compared to 45% of the blocked practice group). Finally, in a study involving 787 pupils from five US schools, interleaved practice of solving maths problems resulted in a much higher score on an unannounced test one month later than blocked practice, with the interleaving group scoring an average of 61% compared to blocked group average of 38% (Rohrer et al., 2020).

5. The benefit of interleaving to problem solving has also been seen in the learning of calculations in science (Samani and Pan, 2021). Here, students completing a university-level physics course studied by solving problems in either blocked or interleaved practice. On a later test, students achieved more correct solutions after having engaged in interleaved practice.

Implementing interleaving in the classroom

Material that requires discrimination

As discussed previously, according to the discriminative-contrast hypothesis, the interleaving effect occurs because mixing up the material helps pupils to notice the differences between the examples or concepts. Therefore, interleaving is most effective when the material being interleaved requires students to note and learn these differences (Birnbaum et al., 2013). Further to this, Firth, Rivers and Boyle (2021), in their review of interleaving as a learning strategy, found that interleaving is of greatest use when differences between items are subtle and where conceptual confusion is likely. Therefore, interleaving is best utilised for similar concepts that students often get confused between.

This also means that interleaving is likely to be most effective within topics, rather than interleaving different topics within a subject (such as one science topic and another separate science topic), or interleaving subjects (such as studying maths, then science, then history).

The concepts are presented alongside one another, with little delay

Again, because discrimination between concepts is crucial to the success of interleaving, it is most effective when these examples are presented alongside one another and without a delay. If the different examples are presented after a delay, it is unlikely that students will be able to hold them in their working memories long enough to contrast them (Kornell and Bjork, 2008).

Interleaving a limited number of brief examples and concepts

In order for students to notice the differences between concepts, these examples must be limited in number and brief (Firth, Rivers and Boyle, 2021). This prevents students' working memories becoming overloaded when trying to recall a large number of different concepts. Keeping the examples brief (for example, using interleaving for vocabulary or categorisation rather than for large ideas such as comparing one whole play or piece of literature to another) again prevents overload and too much of a delay occurring, which would hamper the interleaving effect.

After blocked practice for complex material

As this strategy increases challenge, it may be more beneficial when used with students who have a good level of knowledge and understanding of the content being interleaved, if the content is complex (Perry et al., 2021). This can prevent confusion and frustration from overloading students' working memories with too much new content. This may mean that interleaved practice of different problems, concepts or examples is most beneficial when completed after each of these examples or concepts has been practised in blocked fashion (Hughes and Lee, 2019). Rohrer, Dedrick and Stershic (2015) give the example of students in maths completing blocked problems on the concept or procedure learned that day, before completing interleaved problems of both the concept from that day's learning and those from previous lessons.

Active interleaving

In their study, Carvalho and Goldstone (2015) found that participants performed at a higher level in a later task when interleaving had been *active* rather than passive. For instance, when using interleaving for categorisation learning, it is more effective for students to decide on the correct category assignment rather than passively studying items where the category has been provided. This may also mean that, if used in mathematics, interleaving will be more effective if students practise solving different types of problems as opposed to their teacher explaining or modelling this for them.

Less effective interleaving

The previous discussion shows that interleaving may be ineffective in some circumstances, including:

1. Interleaving different subjects
2. Interleaving large topics, such as studying poetry one lesson and then *Romeo and Juliet* in the next lesson in English literature (that is not to say this won't result in benefits from retrieval practice and spacing!)
3. Interleaving a large number of examples or concepts
4. Leaving a delay between interleaved concepts
5. Only using passive interleaving.

Examples of interleaving in the classroom

*   In science, interleaving can be used to help students learn to categorise intrusive and extrusive igneous rocks by presenting each type of rock in an interleaved fashion and looking at multiple examples of both types of rocks at the same time.

*   Interleaving can be used to help pupils to distinguish between similar vocabulary and concepts in a topic. For example, in biology, pupils can easily confuse the meanings of antigens, antibodies and antibiotics when studying infectious disease. In English, interleaving may help with learning the difference between similar words such as 'affect' and 'effect', and 'allusion' and 'illusion'.

*   In geography, interleaving can help students to correctly classify glaciers, ice shifts and ice fields, by presenting the main characteristics and photographs of each of them at the same time and then asking students to categorise further interleaved examples into the correct category.

*   In primary maths, pupils may do blocked practice of adding, subtracting, multiplying and dividing fractions before attempting interleaved examples.

*   Similarly, interleaving in maths would involve finding areas of squares, circles and rectangles all in the same practice session rather than just working with one type of figure at a time.

*   Interleaving can also take place within topics in maths. Examples of interleaved questions on coordinates include:

    1. The positions of two coordinates are given as (2,5) and (5,8). Find the midpoint between these two points.

2. The positions of two coordinates are given as (2,5) and (5,8). Find the gradient between these two points.

3. The positions of two coordinates are given as (2,5) and (5,8). Find the straight-line equation that connects these two points.

4. The positions of two coordinates are given as (2,5) and (5,8). Find the length of the line that connects these two points.

- Further examples from maths include finding the length of one side, the perimeter and the size of the angles of a triangle, and mixing questions that require students to factorise equations with those that require them to expand equations.

- In PE, when practising different badminton shots (drop, net, smash) students should interleave all of the different types of shot as opposed to practising lots of one type then lots of another.

- Similarly, when practising types of pass in netball, an interleaved schedule may be as follows:

1. Chest pass
2. Bounce pass
3. Shoulder pass
4. Overhead pass
5. Chest pass
6. Bounce pass
7. Shoulder pass
8. Overhead pass.

- In EYFS, interleaving may be used to practise letter formation – for example, by asking children to write one 'p', one 'q' and one 'g' before returning to 'p' again.

- In languages, students can be set interleaved questions on the past, present and future tenses rather than a block of questions on one tense then another.

- In English, when looking at punctuation, interleaving may involve students solving one problem featuring semicolons, then one featuring colons, then another on commas, then back to semicolons, and so on.

Summary

- Interleaving includes the mixing together of different types of concepts or questions within a single practice session.

- Interleaving is a desirable difficulty as the mixing up of concepts or examples is more challenging than blocked practice but may be more effective for learning.

- Interleaving is effective because it increases opportunities to compare examples, and so helps students to discriminate between them.

- Effective and ineffective interleaving is summarised in the table below:

Effective interleaving	Ineffective interleaving
Interleaving material that requires pupils to discriminate between problems/concepts, emphasising differences between them	Interleaving material that requires pupils to only notice similarities between problems/concepts
Interleaving material within a topic that students tend to confuse	Interleaving large topics or subjects, or material that is not related
Presenting the concepts alongside one another with no delay	Leaving large delays in between the concepts
Interleaving a small number of concepts	Trying to interleave too many concepts, overwhelming students' working memories
Interleaving complex material after blocked practice	Interleaving complex tasks or concepts before students' knowledge of these concepts is secure
Active interleaving	Passive interleaving with no student practice

CHAPTER 6
DESIRABLE DIFFICULTY 4: PRACTICE TESTING

What is testing and why is it a desirable difficulty?

Testing, also known as retrieval practice, involves retrieving previously learned information from the long-term memory (Bjork, 1988). This can take many forms including: answering short-answer, longer-answer or multiple-choice questions; short tasks such as fill-in-the-blanks or matching exercises; reproducing the content, for example, in the form of a diagram, mind map or knowledge organiser; or free recall tasks.

The testing effect describes the finding that, in comparison to restudying, engaging in retrieval of previously learned material makes this information more recallable in the future (Bjork, 1975) and so it is more effective for long-term learning and retention (Bjork and Bjork, 2011).

Retrieval practice can be viewed as a desirable difficulty because while generating answers from memory feels more difficult than being presented with the information during restudying, it also leads to more in-depth processing and therefore improved long-term retention (Perry et al., 2021). This is supported by the 'retrieval effort theory' which states that the testing effect results from the effortful processing completed during retrieval (Rowland, 2014).

Testing is also desirable as it can provide feedback to learners on their learning – making them aware of weaknesses in their memory and gaps in their understanding, and so supporting self-monitoring and more effective future study (Bjork and Bjork, 2020).

What research supports practice testing?

The testing effect has been demonstrated in research again and again, for over a hundred years (Karpicke, 2017). For example, in Roediger and Karpicke's (2006) experiment, learners studied text passages followed by either restudying the text three times, restudying twice and taking one test, or taking three tests. In a final test taken one week later, testing resulted in substantially greater retention than restudying.

These findings have been replicated in recent research. For instance, Donoghue and Hattie's (2021) meta-analysis of 242 studies found practice testing to have a large average effect size of 0.74. Furthermore, Yang and colleagues (2021) in their meta-analysis of 222 studies found there to be strong evidence supporting the existence of the testing effect, including for students of all ages and genders and across 18 subjects.

Critically, research has also found the testing effect to occur when used in real classroom settings. Firstly, a recent meta-analysis using only classroom-based research found a large benefit from retrieval practice, including for students of a variety of ages and across different content areas and retrieval and test formats (Agarwal, Nunes and Blunt, 2021). Secondly, the EEF's review into the use of cognitive science approaches in the classroom found retrieval practice to be one of the most cost-effective and impactful strategies teachers can use to aid learning (Perry et al., 2021).

Implementing retrieval practice in the classroom

Successful retrieval practice

In order to be effective, retrieval practice must be, at least in part, successful (Bjork and Bjork, 2020); students must be able to retrieve at least some of the content accurately (Carpenter, Pan and Butler, 2022). This is so they receive the benefits of the retrieval process and gain an improvement in future recall. It also prevents a negative impact on motivation from failure. This can be achieved by ensuring that the delay between the initial learning and the retrieval practice is long enough to allow for some forgetting, but not so long that the material has been completely forgotten (Bjork and Bjork, 2020).

Scaffolded retrieval practice

To ensure students can be successful, retrieval practice may, initially, be scaffolded. This may be more crucial if students have a lower level of prior knowledge, if their initial learning is less secure or if the material is particularly complex. Ways to achieve this include:

1. Using recognition tasks such as matching exercises or fill-in-the-blank tasks.

2. Asking only factual questions.

3. Providing additional guidance to students such as templates or partially completed activities. For example, this may include providing outlines of concept maps that specify the main aspects of the topic and give prompts or questions for students to include (as opposed to completely free recall), or giving students the first letter of the answer during a quiz.

4. Doing the initial retrieval after a shorter delay from initial learning.

5. Giving topics or questions in advance and allowing students to prepare for the retrieval task through independent study.

Diminishing-cues retrieval practice

In diminishing-cues retrieval practice, students are given cues to ensure that the retrieval practice is successful (where this would otherwise be unlikely to be the case). These cues are then reduced over time until students are able to retrieve the content independently. In an experiment, Fiechter and Benjamin (2018) compared the effectiveness of restudy, retrieval practice and diminishing-cues retrieval practice, where participants were not likely to be able to achieve success on 50% or more of the retrieval questions. They found that participants were able to recall 44% more of the information when they used diminishing-cues retrieval compared to standard retrieval practice. It should be noted that where students are likely to be successful, standard retrieval would be more effective. An example of this is giving lots of smaller questions and additional hints to students when they first retrieve a concept, before moving on to more open-ended questions at a later date.

For example, when first retrieving the potential impact of monopoly power on a market in A-level economics, lots of sub-questions would be used to support students' retrieval including:

1. What is the definition of a monopoly?
2. What are the characteristics of a monopoly?
3. Use a diagram to explain the market outcomes under a monopoly.
4. What are the drawbacks of a monopoly (consider efficiency, price, output, deadweight loss)?
5. What are the benefits of a monopoly (consider reinvestment of profits, dynamic efficiency, economies of scale, avoiding duplication of research)?
6. What does the impact of a monopoly depend on?

Overtime, these cues would be removed so that students were just presented with the question 'Evaluate the potential impact of a monopoly'.

Effortful retrieval practice

However, as suggested previously, the level of difficulty must also require effortful attempts to recall information (Perry et al., 2021). This conclusion was supported by Pyc and Rawson (2009) who examined the impact of the level of difficulty of retrieval practice and found that difficult but successful retrieval has a greater impact on long-term learning than easier successful retrieval.

Low hint strength

Giving too strong hints may make the answer to the retrieval practice guessable, and if a student does guess the answer, they have not used their long-term memory and so will not benefit from the testing effect. In contrast, not using hints makes the retrieval practice more difficult, resulting in more in-depth processing and greater gains in long-term retention. Where it is necessary to provide hints (for example, because students will not experience any successful retrieval without them), this should be the fewest possible hints needed to support students, and these hints should also be removed over time. This was supported by Vaughn and colleagues (2022) who found that giving stronger hints during retrieval practice impaired later recall.

For instance, when asking students to first recall the names of bones in PE, giving the first letter of the name may be a useful hint if students would otherwise struggle to recall this. However, giving too many hints, such as 'cla____' for the clavicle or 'hum____' for the humerus bone, may mean students are not retrieving enough of the content themselves.

Feedback on retrieval practice

Feedback on retrieval practice can lead to larger gains in long-term learning than retrieval practice where no feedback is provided. For example, Yang and colleagues' (2021) previously mentioned meta-analysis found that offering feedback following quizzes significantly increases learning, with individual studies also finding that giving feedback after retrieval practice improves results on delayed tests (Vojdanoska, Cranney and Newell, 2010). This is because feedback reveals misconceptions, errors and aspects that students were unable to retrieve accurately or completely and gives students an opportunity to correct them and fill in any knowledge gaps (Rowland, 2014; Perry et al., 2021; Carpenter, Pan and Butler, 2022).

Further important points regarding feedback on retrieval practice include the following:

- Feedback is especially important and makes a larger difference to future retention when initial retrieval performance has been low (Rowland, 2014). Therefore, feedback can be said to overcome unsuccessful retrieval practice.

- Feedback may be more important if pupils get the answer correct but had low confidence in the correctness of the answer, because it helps to reinforce the correct answer in the future. However, not all elements require feedback; feedback on well-known correct answers may be an inefficient use of time.

- Feedback may also help students to develop their metacognition. In a study that compared retrieval practice with feedback to that without, feedback was found to improve participants' ability to identify both correct and incorrect answers. Therefore, this feedback can improve the accuracy of students' judgements of learning (Naujoks, Harder and Händel, 2022).

- To be most effective, students should actively process the feedback by using it to evaluate the correctness of their retrieval practice against the correct answer (Donoghue and Hattie, 2021).

- In order to support the transfer of the material covered in retrieval practice to new contexts, elaborative feedback should be given. This may include explaining why answers are correct or incorrect, restudy or reteaching of the material to be learned, or feedback that includes further explanation (Pan and Rickard, 2018).

Spaced and repeated retrieval practice

Retrieval practice should be spaced from initial learning and repeated over time. According to Bjork and Bjork's New Theory of Disuse (1992), memories have a retrieval strength and a storage strength. Storage strength is the degree to which the information is embedded in the long-term memory – how well learned it is. Retrieval strength is the ease with which the memory can currently be accessed and recalled.

Moreover, the theory explained that there is a negative relationship between retrieval strength and the gains in storage strength that result from retrieving the memory. If retrieval strength is high (for example, because the content has just been studied), there will be less impact on storage strength as it is easy to recall the information and long-term memory is not required. In contrast, if retrieval strength is currently low, there will be larger gains in storage strength when the memory is recalled. This shows that spaced retrieval practice that occurs after a delay (to allow for retrieval strength to fade) and is repeated over time is more effective at increasing storage strength and therefore long-term retention.

There are several other considerations when using spaced retrieval practice, including the following:

1. The delay to retrieval must be long enough to ensure the retrieval is effortful but not so long that no recall is possible. This will depend on the prior knowledge of the students and the complexity of the material. However, after initial learning it may be best to revisit the information between two days and a week, where possible.

2. Three to four repetitions may be most beneficial in ensuring long-term recall (Donoghue and Hattie, 2021).

3. The combination of retrieval practice and spacing form a study method called 'successive relearning'. This involves an initial session in which learners try to retrieve the information they are learning and then receive feedback to check their accuracy. They then repeat the retrieval practice until they are able to recall all of the information correctly. This initial session is followed, after a delay, by further sessions where the learner again attempts to retrieve the information, gains feedback and repeats the retrieval until all of the information can be recalled (Carpenter, Pan and Butler, 2022). The impact of successive relearning has been examined with students using flash cards to carry out retrieval practice and gain immediate feedback. Here, combining practice tests and restudy has led to increased long-term retention (Rawson, Dunlosky and Sciartelli, 2013).

This theory is now supported by further research:

- A meta-analysis of 29 studies on spaced retrieval practice found it to be more effective than massed retrieval practice, with the authors stating that spaced retrieval practice increases the cognitive effort required to complete the retrieval, strengthening the trace in the long-term memory, where massed retrieval practice does not reactivate the trace in the long-term memory (Latimier, Peyre and Ramus, 2021). The study also highlighted the benefit of spaced retrieval practice that varies the conditions under which the retrieval takes place. This means the memory has more contextual cues and so is more likely to be accessible in the future.

- In a recent experiment, 107 students completing an undergraduate college course were given the opportunity to do regular practice tests (Naujoks, Harder and Händel, 2022). They then took a final exam. Students performed better in the end-of-course exam when they completed practice tests, and a larger number of practice tests resulted in a larger final test score.

- A further meta-analysis of 222 studies on retrieval practice found there to be a positive relationship between the number of test repetitions and the testing effect, with larger learning gains coming from repeated tests (Yang et al., 2021).

Retrieval-induced forgetting

Retrieval-induced forgetting refers to the way in which retrieval practice improves the future recall of retrieved items but impairs the recall of other items. Specifically, this occurs with those items (or answers) that are linked to the cues (or questions) used in retrieval practice but are not retrieved, as an alternative answer is retrieved instead. These items suffer reduced retrieval strength as the recalled answer gains retrieval strength instead, making the non-recalled item less accessible in the future (Bjork and Bjork, 1992).

Despite this forgetting, we can relearn the answers that we have not retrieved, and if we do so, the answers will be better remembered than if they were not forgotten in the first place (i.e. more than if the question they are linked to had not been included in retrieval practice). This is due to the low retrieval strength that leads to larger gains in storage strength when the item is relearned (Storm, Bjork and Bjork, 2008). This shows the crucial importance of relearning answers that have not been retrieved, or of restudying all material after retrieval practice. This can be achieved through a schedule of repeated retrieval practice, restudying and thorough feedback.

The most effective format for retrieval practice

As stated at the start of this chapter, retrieval practice can take many forms. A review of the research suggests that the most effective format is dependent firstly on the initial learning material. If the initial learning materials contained additional (or 'seductive') details that students do not need to remember, specific retrieval questions are necessary in retrieval practice in order to help students to remember the more crucial elements and forget the non-crucial information. Free retrieval tasks or general questions should not be used. However, free recall tasks such as 'brain dumps', mind maps or written summaries can be used when no seductive details have been included in the initial learning materials (Eitel, Endres and Renkl, 2022).

Secondly, the most effective format depends on the desired outcomes of the retrieval practice. In a study of the impact of format on the outcomes of retrieval practice, Endres et al. (2020) found that free recall tasks (asking pupils to recall what they remember about a text) led to better later retention of more of the content and increased self-efficacy and interest. This is because students are more likely to feel successful, fostering motivation. However, when using free recall, participants found it harder to judge their learning and identify any missed knowledge. The authors also found that short-answer questions (specific questions on aspects of the text) led to increased retention of the material directly recalled and better metacognitive judgements of learning. This is because they better highlight participants' knowledge gaps or misunderstandings. However, as this meant that participants received negative feedback on their learning from any missed or incorrect answers, feelings of success, and therefore motivation, were lower. This shows that the best format may depend on the amount of initial content students need to retain in the long-term – short-answer questions may be best for smaller amounts of content or for the most crucial elements, whereas free recall may be more beneficial if a wider range of information is required or for the wider knowledge.

Further to this, if the desired outcome is the transfer of test-enhanced learning, this has been shown to occur when broad retrieval formats are used. This includes tasks that require students to construct explanations, asking several questions that address different levels of a concept and free recall tasks (Pan and Rickard, 2018).

Finally, the most effective format may depend on the complexity of the content being retrieved. In a meta-analysis of 118 studies on retrieval practice, Adesope, Trevisan and Sundararajan (2017) found that shorter questions and multiple-choice questions may be more effective for the recall of factual knowledge, while longer-answer questions and more open tasks may be better for larger concepts or more in-depth understanding.

Beyond this, consistent formats – where the format of the retrieval practice is the same as that of the final test – have been shown to be most effective (Yang et al., 2021). This is due to transfer-appropriate processing – the mental processing engaged in during the retrieval practice is the same as that required in the test, increasing later recall (Adesope, Trevisan and Sundararajan, 2017).

Multiple-choice questions in retrieval practice

Multiple-choice questions (MCQs) can form an effective part of retrieval practice. When using MCQs, the following should be noted:

- MCQs can be beneficial as they can improve the recall of untested material, if this is used as an incorrect answer in a question (Bjork, 2011). To achieve this, all alternative answers should be plausible, and it may also be helpful to ask students to explain why the incorrect answers are incorrect.

- MCQs do entail the risk of students remembering false statements as true and so being more likely to choose the same incorrect answers in future tests. For example, a common misconception in science is that the nucleus is 'the brain of the cell' when a more accurate description is that it controls the cell and contains genetic material. If, on an MCQ on the function of the nucleus, students choose the answer saying it is the brain of the cell, they are more likely to remember this again in the future.

- However, this can be overcome by providing feedback. For instance, in a study involving 72 undergraduate students, Butler and Roediger (2008) examined the impact of using MCQs in retrieval practice both with and without feedback. They found that when no feedback was given after the initial MCQ test, there was an increase in the number of incorrect answers students repeated in the final test. However, when feedback was provided, the number of repeated incorrect answers was reduced. Feedback also made participants more likely to choose correct answers again on a future test.

- Confidence-weighted MCQs (where learners choose the answer and indicate how confident they are in comparison to the other options) can enable students to answer related questions more effectively than standard MCQ tests (Sparck, Bjork and Bjork, 2016).

Example MCQ for GCSE business:

Which of the following is the correct definition of variable costs? Select one answer:

- A – Costs that can change over time.
  Why is this answer correct/incorrect?
- B – Costs that do not vary directly with output.
  Why is this answer correct/incorrect?
- C – Costs that vary according to level of output.
  Why is this answer correct/incorrect?
- D – Wages paid to staff for working extra hours.
  Why is this answer correct/incorrect?

Here, answer C is correct. Answer A is incorrect and highlights a common misconception – students often think that variable costs are costs that can change over time rather than with output. Answer B is incorrect and is the definition of a fixed cost, the opposite type of costs that students are required to learn. Finally, answer D is an example of a variable cost but does not cite the definition, as requested by the question.

Covert and overt retrieval practice

Covert retrieval practice occurs when students think of the answer but do not produce information, such as a written response. In overt retrieval practice, students both think of and produce an answer. Studies have shown that covert retrieval can be as effective as overt retrieval. For instance, Smith, Roediger and Karpicke (2013) carried out an experiment in which participants used covert retrieval practice, overt retrieval practice or restudying before sitting a later test. They found that covert retrieval practice increases long-term retention in comparison to restudying and can be as beneficial as overt retrieval practice. Covert retrieval practice may be especially beneficial when students are self-studying, for example, through the use of flash cards. However, a recent study stipulated that in order for covert retrieval to be successful, there must be conditions in place that mean that all students complete the covert retrieval and think about the answer. This may, for example, be achieved by using cold calling after the covert retrieval practice is completed (Sumeracki and Castillo, 2022).

Factual and higher-order retrieval practice

Factual retrieval practice is the retrieval of factual knowledge. For example, in science, when studying energy, factual questions may include 'Name the three states of matter' and 'Draw a particle diagram for a solid'. Higher-order retrieval practice requires pupils to apply their knowledge or perform more complex skills such as analysis, evaluation or comparison. For example, higher-order retrieval practice for the same unit in science may involve asking students to use the particle model to explain how the heating element in the rear window of a car causes the arrangement of ice particles to change as the ice melts. In English, factual retrieval on *Lord of the Flies* may include questions such as 'Give two quotations that hint at the beauty yet danger of the island', whereas higher-order questions may ask students how the novel contributes to an understanding of sanity and of madness, or how the author portrays Ralph's growing understanding of human nature.

Pooja Agarwal (2019) examined the impact of factual and higher-order retrieval practice on higher-order test performance. In her study, high school and college students engaged in retrieval practice with either factual or higher-order questions, or a mix of both. The results showed that both higher-order and mixed retrieval improved later performance on higher-order questions, but factual quizzes did not. This shows that in order to improve higher-order learning, both factual and higher-order questions and tasks should be used as part of retrieval tasks. Higher-order tasks will look different in different year groups and subjects. For example, in art this may include practising complex skills, in science this could be explaining concepts, in maths this may include solving complex problems and in history this may involve source analysis and evaluation questions. Further examples are detailed at the end of this chapter.

Interleaved retrieval practice

As discussed in an earlier chapter, interleaving mixes up questions on related concepts, such as topics that students easily confuse. A recent study by Sana and Yan (2022) demonstrated the potential benefit of interleaved retrieval. Here, students studying a science course took weekly quizzes with either blocked or interleaved questions, sitting a final test four weeks after the course had finished. The researchers found that students performed better on topics that were tested using an interleaved design compared to a blocked design.

An interleaved quiz in business studies may include questions on interest rates and exchange rates, as these are two topics that students often confuse. An example of this is:

1. What are exchange rates?

2. What are interest rates?

3. How are interest rates calculated?

4. How do we use exchange rates to calculate the price of a good in another currency?

5. What impact do increased interest rates have on businesses?

6. What impact do increased exchange rates have on businesses?

In maths, an interleaved quiz can involve mixing up questions on lots of different concepts. An example of this for KS3 maths may include questions on rounding, place value and rules of integers:

1. Round 65.16 to the nearest whole number

2. 74×64

3. 5.8×10

4. Round 5.777 to 2 decimal places

5. $63 + 249$

6. $5.5/10$

7. Round 0.17692 to 3 decimal places

8. 28127–10856

9. 5.54/10

Low stakes

Tests can increase students' feelings of stress and anxiety (Wenzel and Reinhard, 2021). Therefore, it may be important for retrieval practice to be low stakes (when the retrieval practice is not used to assess students' learning).

Summary

Testing involves retrieving previously learned information from long-term memory. It has been shown to be more effective for long-term retention than restudying. According to research:

- The retrieval should be successful but effortful for pupils.
- It is important to give feedback on practice testing, as well as opportunities for pupils to relearn content they did not retrieve.
- Retrieval practice should be spaced from initial learning and repeated over time.
- The most effective format for retrieval practice depends on the initial learning, desired outcomes and the complexity of the material being retrieved.

Case study of retrieval practice at Walton High School

Jade Pearce, director of professional development (formerly assistant headteacher at Walton High School)

Walton High School have utilised the research on retrieval practice to develop a series of principles or 'active ingredients' that we wanted teachers to follow to implement retrieval practice most successfully. This included that retrieval practice should:

1. Be completed from memory
2. Involve all pupils
3. Be low stakes
4. Allow pupils to be successful through effortful work
5. Be supported by corrective feedback
6. Be spaced and repeated
7. Include factual and higher-order questions/tasks.

Departments were then given autonomy to decide what retrieval practice best looks like in their subject. As a result, many different approaches were used by departments across the school. Here are some examples.

Science

A mix of short-answer questions and longer explanation questions were used in science. These quizzes are often completed for homework, and whole-class verbal feedback is provided in the following lesson. For example, when looking at the topic of waves, moving from factual to extended questions includes:

1. What type of wave are sound waves?
2. What type of wave are light waves?
3. State three similarities between light waves and sound waves.
4. State three differences between light waves and sound waves.
5. Describe how radio waves are different from sound waves.
6. Terrestrial television signals and radio signals both use radio waves. Radio signals are transmitted at a longer wavelength than terrestrial television signals. In hilly areas it may be possible to receive radio signals but not receive terrestrial television signals. Explain why.

7. Explain the differences between longitudinal and transverse waves. Your explanation should refer to ultraviolet, ultrasound and seismic waves.

8. Describe the features of ultrasound and X-rays, and what happens to each type of wave after it has entered the human body.

Art

KS3 art retrieval practice includes mark making and how to create visual texture. A main aim of the art department's retrieval practice is encouraging risk and creativity. Therefore, retrieval tasks also give pupils the opportunity to apply previously learned techniques to new tasks. An example of Year 7 retrieval practice on the topic of texture can be seen here and includes opportunities to create different textures.

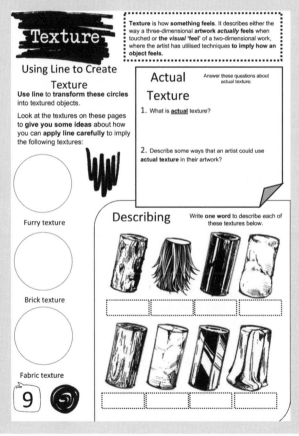

History

The history department uses a range of retrieval techniques including factual questions, source analysis and higher-order questions. Here are examples for the rise of Ho Chi Minh in the form of a mind map:

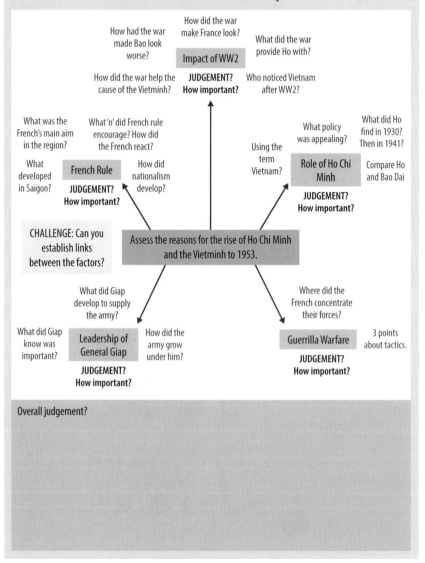

Music

The music department's retrieval practice focuses mainly on vocabulary through the use of weekly definition tests during KS3. An example of a quiz may include:

1. What is meant by the term 'rhythm'?
2. Define the meaning of dynamics.
3. What is the meaning of the term 'harmony'?
4. What is an ensemble?
5. What is a solo?
6. What is a bi-rhythm?
7. What is a riff?

During GCSE music, retrieval practice focuses on set pieces, including asking pupils to compare two set pieces, or to compare one of their set works to a piece of unfamiliar listening.

Maths

Interleaved quizzes that mix questions from different topics form the basis of retrieval practice in maths, with quizzes being completed at the start of each lesson. This also includes a number of higher-order questions that require students to solve a mathematical problem, use multiple aspects of the maths curriculum in one question or, at GCSE, answer exam-style questions. Examples of a maths retrieval practice quiz can be seen below:

1. Express 0.00086 as a number in standard form.
2. If $18 \times 4.3 = 77.4$, what is 180×0.043?
3. A triangle has shorter sides 8cm and 6cm. What is the length of the hypotenuse to 2 decimal places?
4. Calculate the area of a circle with a diameter of 16cm. Give your answer in terms of pi.
5. Find 15% of 130.
6. Explain why we need to have common denominators when we add or subtract fractions.
7. Write 84 as a product of its prime factors.
8. Explain the process of converting a recurring decimal to a fraction.

A further KS3 example can be seen below:

4 Rules Integers ↓	Rounding ↓	BIDMAS ↓	Place Value ↓
1. $63 + 249$	2. Round 65.16 to the nearest whole number	3. $4^2 - 2 \times 3$	4. 5.8×10
5. 74×64	6. Round 5.7777 to 2 d.p	7. $16 \div 2^2 - 1$	8. $5.5 \div 10$
9. $28127 - 10584$	10. Round 0.162779 to 3 d.p	11. $7 + 3 \times 2^2$	12. $5.54 \div 10$

English

Again, in English, retrieval practice takes a range of formats. Factual questions are used to recall knowledge such as vocabulary and details about characters from plays or quotations from texts. Higher-order questions such as how certain themes are demonstrated in texts or plays are used to develop higher-order thinking. Examples of questions may include:

1. What is the definition of the word villain?
2. List three synonyms of the word villain.

3. When does Tybalt call Romeo a villain and why?

4. Explain the extent to which you think Shakespeare presents Tybalt as a villain in the play.

Finally, students are also given the opportunity to practise previously learned skills such as persuasive writing or writing an autobiography. Examples here include:

1. Write a short article for a teenage magazine to give advice to young people on how to handle the stresses of modern life.

2. Write a speech for your class in which you argue that violence is not the solution to conflict.

3. Write a story or personal piece of writing with the title 'The Outsider'.

Computer science

In computer science, retrieval practice includes a heavy emphasis on process questions and completing tasks such as writing a specific algorithm or program. Examples of this for the topic of Programming Fundamentals include:

1. Write an algorithm that will ask the user for their age in years and then print the message 'Happy birthday' many times.

2. Write a line of code that could be used to add the data 'John' to the end of the array.

3. Using pseudocode, create a function that will accept a password string as a parameter passed into the function, returning true if the password is a valid length or false if it is not.

4. Write program code that will generate a random number between 1 and 3.

5. Create an algorithm that will generate a random number between 1 and 3 and then use this to display a message to either walk 10km, run 5km or swim 1km.

Business and economics

The business and economics department use a mix of starter quizzes and homework to carry out retrieval practice, with all homework being discussed in the following lesson. Starter quizzes are used for factual recall such as definitions or stating answers to questions. During homework, students revisit each topic multiple times moving from factual to higher-order questions and finally to case studies or exam-style questions. An example for the topic of market research can be seen below:

1. What is primary market research?

2. What is secondary market research?

3. Give 3 examples of methods used to carry out primary market research

4. Give 3 examples of methods used to carry out secondary market research

5. State one benefit and one drawback to primary market research

6. State one benefit and one drawback to secondary market research

7. Explain why primary market research can give a competitive advantage

8. Explain why secondary market research may not be useful to a business

9. Explain a benefit of quantitative data from market research

10. Read the case study below and justify whether the business owner should use primary or secondary market research

CHAPTER 7

DESIRABLE DIFFICULTIES IN INDEPENDENT STUDY

Use of desirable difficulties by learners

There is a vast amount of research that shows that students do not use desirable difficulties (spacing, testing, interleaving and varying conditions) during independent study, and they often use strategies that have been shown to be less effective instead. The following list summarises a range of examples of this research:

- Rivers' (2021) review of research found that learners do not appreciate the benefits of retrieval practice and do not use it during self-study. In fact, students' judgements of their learning are more favourable to rereading than testing. For instance, the report found that on average only 26% of participants see testing as more effective than rereading and 43% of pupils report rereading as their most used study strategy.

- In an earlier study, when participants read about hypothetical learners preparing for an exam, approximately 70% endorsed rereading, compared to only 30% that endorsed testing (McCabe, 2011). The authors also reported that, when surveyed, students either tended to fail to mention effective techniques or, when the techniques were listed, students ranked them as relatively ineffective.

- A survey of 117 undergraduate students that asked about the strategies used during self-study found rereading was the most popular strategy with 84% of respondents stating they used rereading during self-study and 55% stating it was their first-choice strategy. Further to this, very few (only 11%) used retrieval practice, and of those that did use retrieval practice, most did this to monitor their learning rather than for memory benefits (Karpicke, Butler and Roediger, 2009).

- In an experiment in which students studied using either rereading or testing through flash cards, rereading was rated as more effective, even after students experienced more success with self-testing (Kornell and Son, 2009).

- In a survey carried out by Kornell and Bjork (2007) 86% of students surveyed said that they do not return to material when the course has ended (i.e. they do not use spaced practice). The authors also found that students tended to give higher judgements of learning after massed practice than after spaced practice. They concluded that learners do not believe that spacing is advantageous and so do not use spaced practice to study.

- In Bjork and Kornell's (2008) study of the use of interleaving to learn to categorise paintings by artist, participants consistently reported that blocked practice was more effective than interleaved practice, despite interleaving leading to better performance (Birnbaum et al., 2013).

- Soderstrom and Bjork's (2015) literature review on the distinction between learning and performance found that pupils prefer ineffective strategies such as rereading, massed practice and blocked practice as they feel more effective.

- Surveys have shown that students rate strategies shown by research to be less effective – including rereading, highlighting and recopying notes – as more effective than practice testing (Anthenien et al., 2018).

- Soderstrom and colleagues' (2016) review of the accuracy of judgements of learning (JOLs) made by students highlighted that people give higher JOLs to massed practice and restudying than to spaced practice and retrieval practice.

Why don't students use desirable difficulties in independent study?

Learning versus performance

Performance concerns the gains that occur during initial teaching. It is determined by retrieval strength – the ease with which a memory can be retrieved. In contrast, learning is a permanent change in knowledge and understanding. This is determined by a memory's storage strength – how embedded it is in the long-term memory (Bjork and Bjork, 2011).

This means that the strategies that enhance retrieval strength and performance are different to those that improve storage strength and long-term learning (Bjork, de Winstanley and Storm, 2007). In fact, techniques that enhance long-term learning because they lead to deeper processing and improved encoding often make learning seem more difficult and so impair initial performance (Bjork and Bjork, 2011). For example, massed practice, blocked practice and restudying are likely to lead to improved performance in the short term. However, desirable difficulties such as spaced practice, interleaved practice and retrieval practice are more effective for long-term learning. As students are not often aware of the distinction between performance and learning, they tend to mistake performance for learning, and so use strategies that improve performance but are ineffective for long-term retention (Soderstrom and Bjork, 2015).

This finding is replicated in many papers, for example:

- Bjork and Bjork (2011) reported that blocked practice improves short-term performance more rapidly than interleaved practice and that students misinterpret this improvement as long-term learning, mistaking retrieval strength for storage strength. Therefore, they choose to use blocked practice over interleaved practice, even though interleaving results in much better retention on delayed tests.

- Bjork and Bjork (2020) stated that learners do not want to use interleaving or spacing due to the combination of impaired performance and greater difficulty.

- Hughes and Lee (2019), in a review of all forms of practice, found that interleaving is not as effective as blocked practice for short-term performance and so is less likely to be used by learners.

Inaccurate judgements of learning

It is very difficult to accurately judge learning. This is firstly because we can mistake fluency for understanding or learning, which means that students overestimate the learning that occurs when they use strategies that result in fluency – for example, when rereading (Bjork and Bjork, 2011). Therefore, they use strategies that result in fluency over those that reduce the feeling of fluency but increase long-term retention (those that are desirable difficulties).

Secondly, we can mistake being able to easily recall or retrieve information for learning, but this may be due to the presence of retrieval cues (that may not be available later) or recency (Bjork, 2011). Again, this means that learners will choose strategies that result in easy retrieval over those that increase storage strength, including desirable difficulties.

Both of the above are linked to stability bias – we believe our current recall will remain the same over time and we will be able to retrieve the same amount of information at a later time (Soderstrom and Bjork, 2015). This was supported by Soderstrom, Yue and Bjork (2016) who found that when students are asked to judge their likely ability to recall information at a later date, these judgements lack accuracy as learners use their current level of performance and current ease of retrieval. This means that students believe the gains from strategies such as restudying will be kept in the long-term memory and so choose to use these strategies. Secondly, Carpenter, Pan and Butler (2022) found that students' metacognition is poor as they overestimate their performance in a delayed test.

Students are not aware of effective learning strategies

Further to this, Carpenter, Pan and Butler (2022) stated that learners' metacognitive control is often weak as they do not have the knowledge of effective learning strategies to make good decisions regarding study strategies and so make suboptimal decisions such as using cramming over spacing. This was also found to be true by McCabe (2011) as survey responses showed that students tended to fail to mention effective techniques.

Linked to this, research has shown that students do not know the benefits of testing as a tool for long-term learning, seeing it instead as a strategy for monitoring learning (Bjork and Bjork, 2011).

Attribution error

Attribution error is the way in which we tend to attribute success in learning to ability rather than the activities or strategies utilised during study (Bjork, 2011). This means that if students do experience success through the use of desirable difficulties, they will not necessarily use these strategies again in the future. Similarly, if they experience success due to the use of strategies such as spacing and retrieval in lessons, they may not use these in self-study.

Motivation

According to Chew (2021) one of the main pitfalls that students fall into when they are studying is to use less effective study strategies such as rereading and highlighting because these methods are easy to do. This means that students therefore may lack the motivation to use desirable difficulties.

How can students be encouraged to use desirable difficulties in independent study?

Improving students' knowledge of learning

Students may be more likely to use desirable difficulties if they are aware of effective learning strategies and understand why they are effective (Carpenter, Pan and Butler, 2022). It may be beneficial for students to understand the following:

- How we learn and the simple model of memory (Soderstrom and Bjork, 2015) including working memory and long-term memory, forgetting, encoding and retrieval.

- An understanding of the difference between long-term learning and short-term performance (Kornell and Bjork, 2007), retrieval strength and storage strength, and how the strategies that are most effective for each of these differ.

- An appreciation of effective learning strategies including why they are effective (McCabe, 2011). This should include reference to desirable difficulties and the way in which they lead to deeper processing and improved retention.

Improving students' knowledge of the above can be achieved through teachers explicitly teaching this knowledge to students (Kornell and Bjork, 2007), as well as explicitly teaching students how to use effective revision techniques such as retrieval practice. According to Quigley, Muijs and Stringer's (2018) report on improving students' metacognition and self-regulation, this is necessary as it is unlikely that students will develop effective study strategies independently. The report recommends that this should include:

1. Explicit strategy instruction – explaining how the strategy should be used and why it is effective. For instance, when introducing students to practice testing this may include: defining retrieval practice; informing students of crucial aspects such as getting feedback and spacing and repeating retrieval practice; and giving practical techniques that can be used such as flash cards or quizzes. For interleaving, it may be beneficial to be clear on when interleaving is effective, including topics that are easily confused, categorisation, solving mathematical problems or calculations, and giving examples from different subjects or topics.

2. Modelling of the strategy – the teacher demonstrates how to use the technique themselves.

3. Guided practice – students completing practice with guidance.

4. Independent practice – pupils using the strategy on their own.

It should be noted that the report also recommends that this should be done in the context of specific subjects or topics, rather than just generically, such as through an assembly. It may also be important to share the research that supports these techniques with pupils. McCabe (2011) found that learners are better able to predict the effectiveness of learning strategies, such as those that create desirable difficulties, if they have been exposed to original studies. This could include articles that give an overview of independent study strategies such as Dunlosky's 'Strengthening the student toolbox' (2013), or studies on individual techniques.

There is much support for this approach. For instance, a recent review of spacing and retrieval practice (Carpenter, Pan and Butler, 2022) stated that direct instruction on these strategies, along with the opportunity for students to practise these strategies, can be effective in increasing students' use of them independently. Furthermore, in an experiment where participants were allowed to choose whether they used restudying or testing in independent study, they were much more likely to choose retrieval practice if they had been informed of the benefits of repeated retrieval (including through exposure to specific studies) and were asked to trial retrieval practice (Ariel and Karpicke, 2018).

Giving students experience of desirable difficulties

As well as improving students' knowledge, it may be beneficial for students to experience the impact of effective learning strategies. This can help to foster their appreciation and independent use of these techniques (Bjork, de Winstanley and Storm, 2007).

Again, this is supported by further work. According to Rivers' (2021) review of students' beliefs about practice testing, students need to experience the impact of the most effective strategies on their own memory and learning in order to use them independently. Rivers also recommends ensuring that students compare this impact to the result of using an ineffective strategy such as highlighting. This was replicated by a recent study into how to foster the use of those strategies supported by cognitive science in higher education students (Biwer et al., 2020). Here, students went through a programme designed to improve their knowledge of effective learning strategies and give opportunities to practise their use. This resulted in a positive effect on participants' knowledge and an increased use of strategies including practice testing. Finally, the knowledge, belief, commitment and planning framework (Carpenter, Pan and Butler, 2022) states that as well as delivering direct instruction about effective learning strategies and how to use them, instructors should provide learners with experience of using those strategies in order to increase their belief in their effectiveness.

This can be achieved through teachers setting tasks in lessons or for homework that include, for example, spaced retrieval tasks or interleaved practice.

Making judgements of learning more accurate

It has been shown previously that students' judgements of learning are often inaccurate as they mistake fluency, retrieval strength and short-term performance for long-term learning. This can lead to them overestimating the learning that occurs after ineffective strategies, such as blocked practice or restudying, and underestimating the learning that occurs from strategies such as desirable difficulties that are superior for learning. Therefore, they choose to use these ineffective strategies.

Improving judgements of learning may, consequently, make the use of desirable difficulties more probable. This was shown to be true by Weissgerber and Rummer (2022) in a series of experiments that required participants to prepare for a test using rereading and testing and then estimate their future performance. However, in this case, participants made their judgements of learning after a delay of one or two weeks. When judgements were delayed (so-called 'offline judgements of learning' or 'off-JOLs'), participants rated testing as being more beneficial for learning than rereading. The authors believe this is because judgements that are completed immediately after the use of rereading or testing are biased against testing as participants gain negative feedback regarding their performance; they know some of their responses were incorrect. This does not occur during restudy. This means that learners overestimate their learning and the benefits of restudying, and underestimate the benefits of testing. Therefore, asking students to make judgements of learning after a delay from rereading and testing may be one way to ensure they see testing (and other desirable difficulties) as more effective, which could make them more likely to use these strategies.

Another way to improve the accuracy of judgements of learning may be to give multiple study–test phases (Soderstrom and Bjork, 2015). This is because repeated retrieval opportunities enable students to develop a more accurate idea of their learning, including both correct and incorrect answers.

Motivating students to utilise desirable difficulties

According to Zepeda, Martin and Butler (2020), knowledge of effective learning strategies is not sufficient to ensure learners use these strategies during self-study; we also need to motivate learners to do so. The authors give some suggestions for how this may be achieved, including:

- Making desirable difficulties more enjoyable – for example, by prompting students to do collaborative quizzing.
- Gathering anecdotes or quotes from previous students about how they used strategies including retrieval practice and overcame any costs such as increased study time.
- Attributing success to strategies such as self-testing.
- Giving autonomy over questions, topics, study schedules and tasks.
- Ensuring the appropriate level of difficulty so that students do not give up or see the task as providing little value.
- Giving clear instructions and constructive feedback.

Increasing the use of testing in self-study

More has been written on increasing students' independent use of testing than any other of the desirable difficulties, perhaps due to the huge amount of research that supports the testing effect. As retrieval practice may be most likely to have the largest impact on long-term learning, it may be argued that this is most important. This can be achieved through:

- Making sure learners know they will receive feedback during testing and have an opportunity to restudy (Rivers, 2021). This helps to ensure that they see practice testing as useful and worthwhile.

- Providing students with materials they can use during self-testing such as flash cards or practice questions and answers (Biwer et al., 2020).

- Giving pupils experience of testing (Rivers, 2021) – for example, through using low-stakes quizzes in lessons and setting retrieval tasks for homework. This helps students to experience the impact of retrieval practice and so they are more likely to use it themselves.

Summary

- Research suggests that most students do not use desirable difficulties during independent study, choosing to use less-effective strategies instead.

- This is because students tend to mistake performance for learning, are unable to accurately judge their learning, are unaware of effective study strategies (such as desirable difficulties), attribute future success to ineffective study techniques and are not motivated to use strategies that feel more challenging.

- We can increase the use of desirable difficulties by students by:

  1. Explicitly teaching about learning, memory and effective study techniques.

  2. Ensuring they have experience of these strategies – for example, by setting them for use in homework or using them in lessons.

  3. Making their judgements of learning more accurate – for example, by requiring students to make these judgements after a delay (so techniques that benefit fluency are not favoured).

  4. Motivating students to use these strategies.

Case study of study skills at Walton High School

Jade Pearce, director of professional development (formerly assistant headteacher at Walton High School)

Teachers at Walton High School did lots of work on developing students' independent study skills using multiple approaches. These are outlined below:

1. We used regular assemblies to improve students' knowledge of learning and how to study independently. This included:

   • How we learn according to the cognitive science model of memory, including working and long-term memory, encoding, retrieval and forgetting.

   • The differences between learning and performance, and storage strength and retrieval strength.

   • Spacing – including the spacing effect, Ebbinghaus's Forgetting Curve and examples of how spacing can be achieved in independent study.

   • Testing – including the definition of retrieval practice and the testing effect; references to specific papers that have demonstrated the benefit of retrieval practice over restudying; advice on how to use testing effectively, such as gaining feedback, restudying after retrieval practice and repeating retrieval over time; and examples of how students can implement retrieval practice in self-study including flash cards, quizzes and graphic organisers.

   • Ineffective study strategies – an explanation of why strategies such as highlighting and rereading are less effective for learning, and the research that has demonstrated this.

   • Details on further aspects that are important to effective self-study including sleep, exercise and the use of music and mobile phones.

2. Tutor time was used to give more detailed instruction to students on how to use specific strategies, such as the Leitner system when self-testing using flash cards and when to use specific graphic organisers. This included explicit instruction on the technique, the teacher modelling its use and students carrying out guided and then independent practice.

3. We invited parents to 'parent forums' where they could gain information on how to support their child's learning. This included much of the same information as that given to students in assemblies (on learning, memory, and effective and ineffective learning strategies), but we also gave additional advice on how parents could support this. For example, this included how parents could help their child with retrieval practice and how to create a self-study schedule.

4. In addition to this, individual departments communicated information to parents (for example, through a regular newsletter) on how children could undertake self-study in specific subjects. This included upcoming assessments with links to self-testing questions and answers, online quizzing applications and examples of tasks that were beneficial for students to complete.

5. All departments and teachers provided materials for students to use in self-study that utilised self-testing, interleaving and varied tasks. Examples included retrieval practice work booklets, pre-prepared flash cards and access to online quizzes.

6. All teachers also gave students experience of desirable difficulties including testing, spacing and interleaving in their lessons. Many departments delivered dedicated retrieval lessons, which often started with interleaved quizzes, and homework was often used to set spaced retrieval tasks. While doing this, teachers modelled how techniques should be used in their subject and regularly explained why these strategies are effective and important to students.

7. Older students were encouraged to use any testing done in class to direct further self-study. This was achieved by asking students to note down any topics or aspects that they failed to retrieve in a study log. Students were then expected to do further restudy and retrieval on these areas outside of lesson time. They logged this and any study materials were then checked by the class teacher in a later lesson.

CLOSING REMARKS

Desirable difficulties have the power to improve both teacher instruction and students' independent study and so have a dramatic impact on learning and outcomes. However, as their name suggests, and as we have demonstrated throughout this book, this is not always easy.

Many teachers are familiar with these strategies and may have tried to implement them for the benefit of their students to varying degrees of success. We hope that reading this book has given teachers and school leaders clear and actionable advice for how to successfully implement each of the desirable difficulties 'in action' and how to encourage students to use them effectively outside of lessons.

REFERENCES

Adesope, O. O., Trevisan, D. A. and Sundararajan, N. (2017) 'Rethinking the use of tests: A meta-analysis of practice testing.' *Review of Educational Research*, 87(3), pp. 659–701.

Agarwal, P. K. (2019) 'Retrieval practice & Bloom's taxonomy: Do students need fact knowledge before higher order learning?' *Journal of Educational Psychology*, 111(2), pp. 189–209.

Agarwal, P. K., Nunes, L. D. and Blunt, J. R. (2021) 'Retrieval practice consistently benefits student learning: A systematic review of applied research in schools and classrooms.' *Educational Psychological Review*, 33, pp. 1409–1453.

Alonso, M.-Á. and Fernández, Á. (2011) 'Effects of initial context processing on long-term memory.' *PsyEcology*, 2(1), pp. 75–86.

Anthenien, A. M., DeLozier, S. J., Neighbors, C. and Rhodes, M. G. (2018) 'College student normative misperceptions of peer study habit use.' *Social Psychology of Education*, 21, pp. 303–322.

Ariel, R. and Karpicke, J. D. (2018) 'Improving self-regulated learning with a retrieval practice intervention.' *Journal of Experimental Psychology: Applied*, 24(1), pp. 43–56.

Birnbaum, M. S., Kornell, N., Bjork, E. L. and Bjork, R. A. (2013) 'Why interleaving enhances inductive learning: The roles of discrimination and retrieval.' *Memory & Cognition*, 41(3), pp. 392–402.

Biwer, F., oude Egbrink, M. G. A., Aalten, P. and de Bruin, A. B. H. (2020) 'Fostering effective learning strategies in higher education – a mixed-methods study.' *Journal of Applied Research in Memory and Cognition*, 9(2), pp. 186–203.

Bjork, R. (1975) 'Retrieval as a memory modifier: An interpretation of negative recency and related phenomena.' In R. L. Solso (ed.) *Information Processing and Cognition: The Loyola Symposium*. Lawrence Erlbaum, pp. 123–144.

Bjork, R. A. (1988) 'Retrieval practice and the maintenance of knowledge.' In M. M. Gruneberg, P. E. Morris and R. N. Sykes (eds.) *Practical Aspects of Memory II*. London: Wiley, pp. 396–401.

Bjork, R. A. (2011) 'On the symbiosis of remembering, forgetting, and learning.' In A. S. Benjamin (ed.) *Successful Remembering and Successful Forgetting: A Festschrift in Honor of Robert A. Bjork*. London: Psychology Press, pp. 1–22.

Bjork, R. and Bjork, E. (1992) 'A new theory of disuse and an old theory of stimulus fluctuation.' In A. F. Healy, S. M. Kosslyn, and R. M. Shiffrin (eds.) *From Learning Theory to Connectionist Theory: Essays in Honor of William K. Estes, Volume 2*, pp. 35–68.

Bjork, E. and Bjork, R. (2011) 'Making things hard on yourself, but in a good way: creating desirable difficulties to enhance learning.' In M. A. Gernsbacher, R. W. Pew, L. M. Hough and J. R. Pomerantz (eds.) *Psychology and the Real World: Essays Illustrating Fundamental Contributions to Society*, pp. 59–68.

Bjork, R. A. and Bjork, E. L. (2020) 'Desirable difficulties in theory and practice.' *Journal of Applied Research in Memory and Cognition*, 9(4), pp. 475–479.

Bjork, E. L., de Winstanley, P. A. and Storm, B. C. (2007) 'Learning how to learn: Can experiencing the outcome of different encoding strategies enhance subsequent encoding?' *Psychonomic Bulletin & Review*, 14, pp. 207–211.

Brunmair, M. and Richter, T. (2019) 'Similarity matters: A meta-analysis of interleaved learning and its moderators.' *Psychological Bulletin*, 145(11), pp. 1029–1052.

Butler, A. C. and Roediger, H. L. (2008) 'Feedback enhances the positive effects and reduces the negative effects of multiple-choice testing.' *Memory & Cognition*, 36(3), pp. 604–616.

Carpenter, S., Pan, S. and Butler, A. (2022) 'The science of effective learning with spacing and retrieval practice.' *Nature Reviews Psychology*, 1, pp. 496–511.

Carvalho, P. F. and Goldstone, R. L. (2015) 'The benefits of interleaved and blocked study: Different tasks benefit from different schedules of study.' *Psychonomic Bulletin & Review*, 22, pp. 281–288.

Cepeda, N. J. et al. (2008) 'Spacing effects in learning: a temporal ridgeline of optimal retention.' *Psychological Science*, 19(11), pp. 1095–1102.

Chen, O., Castro-Alonso, J. C., Paas, F. and Sweller, J. (2018) 'Undesirable difficulty effects in the learning of high-element interactivity materials.' *Frontiers in Psychology*, 9: 1483.

Chen, O., Paas, F. and Sweller, J. (2021) 'Spacing and interleaving effects require distinct theoretical bases: A systematic review testing the cognitive load and discriminative-contrast hypotheses.' *Educational Psychology Review*, 33(4), pp. 1499–1522.

Chew, S. L. (2021) 'An advance organizer for student learning: Choke points and pitfalls in studying.' *Canadian Psychology/Psychologie Canadienne*, 62(4), pp. 420–427.

Donoghue, G. and Hattie, J. (2021) 'A meta-analysis of ten learning techniques.' *Frontiers in Education*, 6.

Dunlosky, J. (2013) 'Strengthening the student toolbox: Study strategies to boost learning.' *American Educator*, 37(3), pp. 12–21.

Eitel, A., Endres, T. and Renkl, A. (2022) 'Specific questions during retrieval practice are better for texts containing seductive details.' *Applied Cognitive Psychology*, 36(5), pp. 996–1008.

Endres, T., Kranzdorf, L., Schneider, V. and Renkl, A. (2020) 'It matters how to recall – task differences in retrieval practice.' *Instructional Science*, 48, pp. 699–728.

Fiechter, J. L. and Benjamin, A. S. (2018) 'Diminishing-cues retrieval practice: A memory-enhancing technique that works when regular testing doesn't.' *Psychonomic Bulletin Review*, 25(5), pp. 1868–1876.

Firth, J., Rivers, I. and Boyle, J. (2021) 'A systematic review of interleaving as a concept learning strategy.' *Review of Education*, 9(2), pp. 642–684.

Gick, M. L. and Holyoak, K. J. (1980) 'Analogical problem solving.' *Cognitive Psychology*, 12(3), pp. 306–355.

Goossens, N. A. et al. (2016) 'Distributed practice and retrieval practice in primary school vocabulary learning: A multi-classroom study.' *Applied Cognitive Psychology*, 30(5), pp. 700–712.

Hall, K. G., Domingues, D. A. and Cavazos, R. (1994) 'Contextual interference effects with skilled baseball players.' *Perceptual and Motor Skills*, 78(3), pp. 835–841.

Homa, D. and Cultice, J. C. (1984) 'Role of feedback, category size, and stimulus distortion on the acquisition and utilization of ill-defined categories.' *Journal of Experimental Psychology: Learning, Memory, and Cognition*, 10(1), pp. 83–94.

Honzik, C. H. and Tolman, E. C. (1936) 'The perception of spatial relations by the rat: A type of response not easily explained by conditioning.' *Journal of Comparative Psychology*, 22(2), pp. 287–318.

Hughes, C. A. and Lee, J.-Y. (2019) 'Effective approaches for scheduling and formatting practice: Distributed, cumulative, and interleaved practice.' *Teaching Exceptional Children*, 51(6), pp. 411–423.

Isarida, T. and Isarida, T. (2004) 'Effects of environmental context manipulated by the combination of place and task on free recall.' *Memory*, 12(3), pp. 376–384.

Kang, S. H. K. and Pashler, H. (2012) 'Learning painting styles: Spacing is advantageous when it promotes discriminative contrast.' *Applied Cognitive Psychology*, 26(1), pp. 97–103.

Karpicke, J. D. (2017) 'Retrieval-based learning: A decade of progress.' In J. T. Wixted (ed.) *Cognitive Psychology of Memory, Vol. 2 of Learning and Memory: A comprehensive reference* (J. H. Byrne, series ed.). Oxford: Academic Press, pp. 487–514.

Karpicke, J. D., Butler, A. C. and Roediger, H. L. (2009) 'Metacognitive strategies in student learning: Do students practise retrieval when they study on their own?' *Memory*, 17(4), pp. 471–479.

Karpicke, J. D. and O'Day, G. M. (in press) 'Elements of effective learning.' In M. J. Kahana and A. D. Wagner (eds.) *The Oxford Handbook of Human Memory, Volume II: Applications*. Oxford University Press.

Kornell, N. and Bjork, R. A. (2007) 'The promise and perils of self-regulated study.' *Psychonomic Bulletin & Review*, 14(2), pp. 219–224.

Kornell, N. and Bjork R. A. (2008) 'Learning concepts and categories: Is spacing the "enemy of induction"?' *Psychological Science*, 19(6): pp. 585–592.

Kornell, N. and Son, L. (2009) 'Learners' choices and beliefs about self-testing.' *Memory*, 17(5), pp. 493–501.

Latimier, A., Peyre, H. and Ramus, F. (2021) 'A meta-analytic review of the benefit of spacing out retrieval practice episodes on retention.' *Educational Psychology Review*, 33, pp. 959–987.

Mannes, S. M. and Kintsch, W. (1987) 'Knowledge organization and text organization.' *Cognition and Instruction*, 4(2), pp. 91–115.

McCabe, J. (2011) 'Metacognitive awareness of learning strategies in undergraduates.' *Memory & Cognition*, 39(3), pp. 462–476.

Naujoks, N., Harder, B. and Händel, M. (2022) 'Testing pays off twice: Potentials of practice tests and feedback regarding exam performance and judgment accuracy.' *Metacognition and Learning*, 17, pp. 479–498.

Pan, S. C. and Rickard, T. C. (2018) 'Transfer of test-enhanced learning: Meta-analytic review and synthesis.' *Psychological Bulletin*, 144(7), pp. 710–756.

Perry, T. et al. (2021) *Cognitive science in the classroom*. London: Education Endowment Foundation (EEF).

Postman, L. and Tuma, A. H. (1954) 'Latent learning in human subjects.' *The American Journal of Psychology*, 67(1), p. 119–123.

Pyc, M. A. and Rawson, K. A. (2009) 'Testing the retrieval effort hypothesis: Does greater difficulty correctly recalling information lead to higher levels of memory?' *Journal of Memory and Language*, 60(4), pp. 437–447.

Quigley, A., Muijs, D. and Stringer, E. (2018) *Metacognition and self-regulated learning: guidance report*. London: EEF.

Rawson, K. A., Dunlosky, J. and Sciartelli, S. M. (2013) 'The power of successive relearning: Improving performance on course exams and long-term retention.' *Educational Psychology Review*, 25, pp. 523–548.

Rivers, M. L. (2021) 'Metacognition about practice testing: A review of learners' beliefs, monitoring, and control of test-enhanced learning.' *Educational Psychology Review*, 33(3), pp. 823–862.

Roediger, H. L. and Karpicke, J. D. (2006) 'Test-enhanced learning: Taking memory tests improves long-term retention.' *Psychological Science*, 17(3), pp. 249–255.

Roediger, H. L. and Karpicke, J. D. (2011) 'Intricacies of spaced retrieval: A resolution.' In A. S. Benjamin (ed.) *Successful Remembering and Successful Forgetting: A Festschrift in Honor of Robert A. Bjork*. Psychology Press, pp. 23–47.

Rohrer, D. (2012) 'Interleaving helps students distinguish among similar concepts.' *Educational Psychology Review*, 24, pp. 355–367.

Rohrer, D., Dedrick, R. F. and Stershic, S. (2015) 'Interleaved practice improves mathematics learning.' *Journal of Educational Psychology*, 107(3), pp. 900–908.

Rohrer, D., Dedrick, R. F., Hartwig, M. K. and Cheung, C.-N. (2020) 'A randomized controlled trial of interleaved mathematics practice.' *Journal of Educational Psychology*, 112(1), pp. 40–52.

Rohrer, D. and Taylor, K. (2007) 'The shuffling of mathematics problems improves learning.' *Instructional Science*, 35, pp. 481–498.

Rowland, C. A. (2014) 'The effect of testing versus restudy on retention: A meta-analytic review of the testing effect. *Psychological Bulletin*, 140(6), pp. 1432–1463.

Samani, J. and Pan, S. C. (2021) 'Interleaved practice enhances memory and problem-solving ability in undergraduate physics.' *npj Science of Learning*, 6, 32.

Sana, F. and Yan, V. X. (2022) 'Interleaving retrieval practice promotes science learning.' *Psychological Science*, 33(5), pp. 782–788.

Smith, M. A., Roediger, H. L. and Karpicke, J. D. (2013) 'Covert retrieval practice benefits retention as much as overt retrieval practice.' *Journal of Experimental Psychology: Learning, Memory, and Cognition*, 39(6), pp. 1712–1725.

Soderstrom, N. C. and Bjork, R. A. (2015) 'Learning versus performance: An integrative review.' *Perspectives on Psychological Science*, 10(2), pp. 176–199.

Soderstrom, N. C., Yue, C. L. and Bjork, E. L. (2016) 'Metamemory and education.' In J. Dunlosky and S. K. Tauber (eds.) *The Oxford Handbook of Metamemory*. Oxford: Oxford University Press, pp. 197–215.

Sparck, E. M., Bjork, E. L. and Bjork, R. A. (2016) 'On the learning benefits of confidence-weighted testing.' *Cognitive Research: Principles and Implications*, 1, 3.

Stevenson, H. W. (1954) 'Latent learning in children.' *Journal of Experimental Psychology*, 47(1), pp. 17–21.

Storm, B. C., Bjork, E. L. and Bjork, R. A. (2008) 'Accelerated relearning after retrieval-induced forgetting: The benefit of being forgotten.' *Journal of Experimental Psychology: Learning, Memory, and Cognition*, 34(1), pp. 230–236.

Sumeracki, M. A. and Castillo, J. (2022) 'Covert and overt retrieval practice in the classroom.' *Translational Issues in Psychological Science*, 8(2), pp. 282–293.

Sweller, J. (2010) 'Element interactivity and intrinsic, extraneous, and germane cognitive load.' *Educational Psychology Review*, 22, pp. 123–138.

Taylor, K. and Rohrer, D. (2010) 'The effects of interleaved practice.' *Applied Cognitive Psychology*, 24(6), pp. 837–848.

Vaughn, K. E. et al. (2022) 'The effect of hint strength on the benefits of retrieval practice.' *Applied Cognitive Psychology*, 36(2), pp. 468–476.

Verkoeijen, P. P., Rikers, R. M. and Schmidt, H. G. (2005) 'Limitations to the spacing effect.' *Experimental Psychology*, 52(4), pp. 257–263.

Vlach, H. A. and Sandhofer, C. M. (2013) 'Retrieval dynamics and retention in cross-situational statistical word learning.' *Cognitive Science*, 38(4), pp. 757–774.

Vojdanoska, M., Cranney, J. and Newell, B. (2010) 'The testing effect: The role of feedback and collaboration in a tertiary classroom setting.' *Applied Cognitive Psychology*, 24(8), pp. 1183–1195.

Weissgerber, S. C. and Rummer, R. (2022) 'More accurate than assumed: Learners' metacognitive beliefs about the effectiveness of retrieval practice.' *Learning and Instruction*, 83, 101679.

Wenzel, K. and Reinhard, M.-A. (2021) 'Learning with a double-edged sword? Beneficial and detrimental effects of learning tests—taking a first look at linkages among tests, later learning outcomes, stress perceptions, and intelligence.' *Frontiers in Psychology*, 12.

Willingham, D. T. (2009) *Why Don't Students Like School?: A Cognitive Scientist Answers Questions About How the Mind Works and What It Means for the Classroom.* San Francisco: Jossey-Bass.

Yang, C. et al. (2021) 'Testing (quizzing) boosts classroom learning: A systematic and meta-analytic review.' *Psychological bulletin*, 147(4), pp. 399–435.

Zepeda, C. D., Martin, R. S. and Butler, A. C. (2020) 'Motivational strategies to engage learners in desirable difficulties.' *Journal of Applied Research in Memory and Cognition*, 9(4), pp. 468–474.